"*Freedom, Justice, and Decolonization* is a tour de force written by one of the most brilliant and visionary philosophers of our time. This book has never been more relevant at a time when millions have suffered through a terrifying pandemic and then cheered at the courageous and necessary challenge to anti-black racism in the streets of almost every city and town in the United States. In accordance with the mandate to shift the geographies of reason Gordon foregrounds philosophies and political theories of the Global South but only to broaden the reach of such endeavors to move to a universality not bogged down by the violence of colonialism. The great ideals of dignity, freedom, liberation, and justice are defended on every page infused with the lessons and demands of emancipation that inhere in the struggles for decolonization. This is not a trendy book that tries to show us that we have grown out of the great dream of a new species of humanity to use Fanon's telling phrase. The opposite is the case; it calls us and inspires us to fight on for the new 'species.' This book is a must read for anyone who wants to understand the complexities of our time and cherishes the hope that we can create a world worthy of the ideas Gordon eloquently defends."

Drucilla Cornell, Research Professor, University of
Venda, Professor Emerita at Rutgers University

"If you are interested in enlarging the scope of not just knowledge, but also your curiosity in the discipline of philosophy as not just a 'stand-in and inter-preter' but instead the fluctuating plane interwoven in 'shifting the geography of reason,' you need to read this book. If you are interested in what can be learned about the connections between what we are used to thinking and our very different ways of thinking, you need to read this book. If you think that 'cultural politics,' 'multiculturalism,' 'diversity,' and 'tolerance' are overused and misused words, you need to read this book. If you are overwhelmed by 'pessimism of the intellect' and hope for some 'optimism of the will,' you need to read this book. Lastly, since you are not going to be traveling so much in the future, maybe you can travel in the different landscapes and different exchanges, by reading this book."

Natalija Mićunović, Institute of Social
Sciences, Belgrade, Serbia

"In *Freedom, Justice, and Decolonization*, Gordon offers a profound and challenging discussion of topics both abstract and immediate to make a case for the pressing need for a radical and wide-ranging project of decolonization. In so doing, he undertakes a daring and exciting re-orientation of our approach to such staid and often threadbare preoccupations as freedom, rationality, essence, justice, and the political, each of which is in desperate need of decolonizing. All of this is, at the same time, interwoven with engaging and challenging meditations on pressing issues ranging from the political situation in contemporary

Russia, to the pragmatics of Black liberation in the U.S., to the uses and abuses of Afropessimism in and beyond the academy. The result is vibrant and exhilarating demonstration of the power of human *thought* in a political and cultural moment that consistently works to negate it."

Michael Monahan, author of *The Creolizing Subject* and editor of *Creolizing Hegel*

"In this deeply, prognostic reflection, Lewis R. Gordon expounds eloquently on the struggles for freedom, justice, and decolonization from a Black existentialist perspective. By shifting the geography of reason, prioritizing the responsibility of reason, and insisting on reasonability, his powerful critique of moralism and liberalism moves through paradoxes of political commitment and contemporary forms of decadence – Euromodernity, presumptions of justice, secularized theodicies, Afropessimism, and postmodern avowals. The remarkable site he delivers for political responsibility produces actions that reach beyond the self to the anonymous 'we.' There, in this space of the yet-to-be-born and of many who have become ancestors, he offers a future that is never ours, and presents an unexpected but profound understanding of political responsibility that is premised on a political form of love."

Nkiru Uwechia Nzegwu, SUNY Distinguished Professor

Freedom, Justice, and Decolonization

The eminent scholar Lewis R. Gordon offers a probing meditation on freedom, justice, and decolonization. What is there to be understood and done when it is evident that the search for justice, which dominates social and political philosophy of the North, is an insufficient approach for the achievements of dignity, freedom, liberation, and revolution? Gordon takes the reader on a journey as he interrogates a trail from colonized philosophy to re-imagining liberation and revolution to critical challenges raised by Afropessimism, theodicy, and looming catastrophe. He offers not forecast and foreclosure but instead an urgent call for dignifying and urgent acts of political commitment. Such movements take the form of examining what philosophy means in Africana philosophy, liberation in decolonial thought, and the decolonization of justice and normative life. Gordon issues a critique of the obstacles to cultivating emancipatory politics, challenging reductionist forms of thought that proffer harm and suffering as conditions of political appearance and the valorization of nonhuman being. He asserts instead emancipatory considerations for occluded forms of life and the irreplaceability of existence in the face of catastrophe and ruin, and he concludes, through a discussion with the Circassian philosopher and decolonial theorist, Madina Tlostanova, with the project of shifting the geography of reason.

Lewis R. Gordon is Professor and Head of the Department of Philosophy at the University of Connecticut at Storrs; Honorary President of the Global Center for Advanced Studies; Honorary Professor in the Unit for the Humanities at Rhodes University, South Africa; Chairperson of the American Philosophical Association Committee on Public Philosophy; and Chairperson of the Awards Committee and Global Collaborations for the Caribbean Philosophical Association, of which he was the organization's first president. His books published by Routledge include *Fanon and the Crisis of European Man, Existence in Black, Existentia Africana, Disciplinary Decadence*, and, with Jane Anna Gordon, *Not Only the Master's Tools* and *Of Divine Warning*.

Freedom, Justice, and Decolonization

Lewis R. Gordon

Routledge
Taylor & Francis Group

NEW YORK AND LONDON

First published 2021
by Routledge
52 Vanderbilt Avenue, New York, NY 10017

and by Routledge
2 Park Square, Milton Park, Abingdon, Oxon, OX14 4RN

Routledge is an imprint of the Taylor & Francis Group, an informa business

Library of Congress Cataloging-in-Publication Data
A catalog record for this title has been requested

ISBN: 978-0-367-63296-0 (hbk)
ISBN: 978-0-367-63246-5 (pbk)
ISBN: 978-1-003-11259-4 (ebk)

Typeset in Bembo
by KnowledgeWorks Global Ltd.

To my grandmothers Gertrude and Sylvia

Contents

Preface, with Acknowledgments

I here offer some of my recent thought on freedom, justice, and decolonization. The first and second concepts are discussed much in professional philosophy, and the third, although gathering momentum in debates across the Global South, is often avoided in the Global North because of the unfortunate investments in ongoing colonial relations on which that geopolitical designation gained much of its power. I offer this book with the aim of providing its readers with some critical resources with which to address this unfortunate historical circumstance.

A good number of my writings pertain to a variety of disciplines. A hallmark of their critical position is from the meeting of existence and challenges to its livability posed by forces of oppression. This book is, thus, to some extent, reflections on freedom, justice, and decolonization from the perspective of Black existentialism. In that regard, they offer critiques of philosophy and a variety of theoretical perspectives in which presuppositions of Black irrelevance prevail. Still, there is no greater fear from proponents of such claims than encountering their own irrelevance. Thus, instead of being reactive, the task at hand is to press on and address issues that, at least from intellectual movements such as Africana philosophy and Black existentialism, are highly relevant. The reader can, through exploring what unfolds, decide as well on whether these ideas are useful.

I conclude through a conversation with the famed decolonial philosopher Madina Vladimirovna Tlostanova. She, along with the organizing committee of the NOW-2: CONSTRUCTING CONTEMPORANEITY festival, arranged for me to discuss my ideas with Russian dissidents in 2018. The Heinrich Böll Foundation and public media resource Colta.ru made that meeting possible. Herself Uzbek-Cherkess and, thus, a member of one of Russia's racially marked minorities, Tlostanova is among those philosophers, decolonial theorists, and feminists for whom concerns of racial invisibility are at the forefront of their analysis. A short version of our conversation was published in Russian in the journal *Colta* under the title: "Луис Гордон: «Высокомерное заблуждение всех империй в том, что они открывают двери в одну сторону»" ("Lewis Gordon: 'the arrogance of all empires is that they imagine they could open doors that lead one-way'"), with excerpts appearing here and there in such forums as South Africa's *The New Frame* and the American Philosophical Association's Blog Series *Black Issues in Philosophy*. It appears here in its entirety.

Given the unfortunate history of the Russian government's fomenting white supremacy in its destabilization efforts across the globe under Vladimir Putin's leadership, one could imagine the plight of that country's racial minorities and political dissidents. It was important for me to visit there, with its contradictions, as it continues to be necessary to reach out for connection among dissidents across the globe. Indeed, I made it a point of visiting authoritarian countries over the past three decades in solidarity with people fighting against state-level efforts to crush their spirit. The reader will notice the presence of debates and ideas from across the globe, though especially the Global South, in the chapters that precede this concluding discussion and also the importance of such thought for the discussion of these two philosophers, Tlostanova and me—one, a woman of color from Russia living in Sweden; another, a man of color, born in Jamaica and a citizen of the United States. Both of us understand we are part of struggles much greater than ourselves. As with the preceding discussions, the aim is for our conversation to offer sustenance for those thinking what needs to be thought to fight the proverbial good fight.

In addition to Russia, the chapters in this book were presented in Antigua, Argentina, Australia and Tasmania, Brazil, Canada, Colombia, Denmark, France, Germany, India, Italy, Jamaica, Kenya, Mexico, New Zealand, Peru, Portugal, Senegal, Serbia, Slovenia, South Africa, Sweden, the U.S. Virgin Islands of St. Croix and St. Thomas, and the United Kingdom. Early versions appeared in *Contemporary Political Theory, International Journal of Diversity Studies, Listening, Social Alternations,* and *The South Atlantic Quarterly.* I thank the academics, artists, community activists, and audiences in those countries for their valuable feedback and those journals for permission to offer elaborated, revised versions here. Responsibility for the form in which these ideas are offered here is, of course, mine.

As always, appreciation and love go to my family Jane Anna Gordon, Elijah Gordon, Jennifer Gordon and Luis Peña Ortiz, Mathieu Gordon and Donnielle Fitzgerald, and Sula Gordon, one of whose paintings grace the cover of this book, and Simeon Gamesu Kobla Mark Cofie, all of whom continue to make my life worth living. This is no understatement, as the completion of this book was interrupted by my struggle with COVID-19, the disease brought on through infection from the novel coronavirus, over the course of several months. I write this preface with gratitude for my continued convalescence and in the midst of lamenting the loss of so many people, personal and unknown, from this deadly affliction, and the multiple converging pandemics of colonialism and racism that took so many to the streets after witnessing 8 minutes and 46 seconds of a cruel police officer's knee on George Floyd's neck in Minneapolis, Minnesota. To the families of the dead, I offer my condolence, and to those continuing the fight, I offer my solidarity and commitment in struggle against the nefarious forces, whose incompetence and maleficence exacerbated the deadly consequences of the pandemic and against whom we must all continue to fight for the sake of dignity, freedom, and lives worth living.

Chapter 1

On Philosophy,
in Africana Philosophy

To begin, I would like to declare that this book is not written from the perspective of a philosophy nationalist. By this, I mean that although philosophy often illuminates reality, it is not the sole means of doing so. What is today sometimes called disciplinary and epistemic arrogance is a vice that impedes clear thinking and produces dysfunctional attitudes and a declining relationship with reality. Many considerations, disciplines, and ways of living, affectively and epistemologically, offer much for such an ultimately infinite virtuous task. There is always something to learn from different ways of learning, knowing, expressing, and living. This is not to say that philosophy lacks its moments. Quite a bit of those will inform much of the discussion that will follow, although, to stress, not exclusively so. Let us proceed, then, with some reflections on philosophy from issues posed by it and its creolized hybrid—namely, Africana or African diasporic philosophy—as freedom, justice, and decolonization are central concerns of that area of thought.

The reader may be immediately struck by the expression "creolized hybrid." "Creolized" in this context refers to bringing at times opposing forces into living mixtures or syntheses.[1] Announcing a creolized element does not reject the possibility of a prior creolized form, however, since, as these reflections will show, I do not presume an initial African "purity." As the human being is the quintessential creature of metastability—that is, elusive of being pinned down under an essence—the solace of being onto itself, of being out of relations with all others, though often a wish of some philosophers, is a luxury or preemption that is not Africana peoples'. Africa as humanity's birthplace means the upsurge of self-consciousness was, as well, that of a reaching for which our species has its proverbial ongoing journey. There is a poetic irony here, since a well-known prejudice, since the rise of Euromodern worldviews, is that thought was sparked in Asia and matured in Europe; consciousness in Africa was, thus, a supposed import from the Northern East and West. This unfortunate presumption elides the significance of the continent's name in one of its ancient tongues—Mdw Ntr (also known as Medu Neter, the language of Kmt, or ancient Egypt)—which amounts to turning toward the opening of the birthplace or womb of humanity (*af-rui-ka*, "turning toward the opening of the *ka*").[2] The peculiarly gendered, psychoanalytical significance of subsequent denying or at least forgetting of humanity's primordial womb speaks, proverbially, volumes.[3] So, let us turn our attention to some erasure, forgetting, denial, and, as each falls under the weight of critique, remembering.

"Philosophy," conventional wisdom has it, began in Ancient Greece. A problem with that claim is that an accepted view is not necessarily a correct one. A moment's reflection on the word, its history, and the political circumstances leading to its reception should occasion a long pause. "Greeks," after all, was the Roman name for the broad range of people who spoke varieties of the Greek language. Most of the people ascribed as such referred to themselves as Hellenes and much of the land of Greece today, including areas of western Turkey, was known as Hellas. Beyond that, Greek-speaking people included northern Africans, western Asians, and southern peoples, of what is later known as Europe. As the presumption among subsequent early Euromodern and later German Enlightenment scholars was that the earliest practice of philosophy was among the ancient Athenians, the term acquired a near sacred association with Hellenic peoples. Understanding that the Hellenes were but one group among other Greek-speaking peoples to have emerged in antiquity reveals the fallacy. It is as if to call English-speaking peoples of the present "English." The confusion should be evident. A product of Euromodern imagination, with a series of empires laying claim to the coveted metonymic intellectual identity for posterity, Ancient Greeks stand as a supposed "miracle" from which a hitherto "dark" and presumably intellectually-limited shell of humanity fell sway to what eventually became, through Latin, "civilization."[4]

"Human beings," *Homo sapiens*, have been around for about 220,000—possibly 300,000—years, and evidence of intellectual leaps abound throughout. A fragile species at times facing extinction, what has secured human survival is intelligence with, of course, quite a bit of luck. The idea that our species remained limited until we reached the shores of the Mediterranean Sea is far-fetched. More, a few thousand years of writings before those inscribed in Greek should not be ignored. If they were not the beginning, on whose ideas did ancient Greek-speaking people's reflections rested? The obvious answer is *their ancients*, and for them, as for those of us today who sift through the past, we should bear in mind that they were both not "us" and "us." They were not us in the sense of a single line of cultural inheritance; yet they were "us" in that their achievements belong to all of us, to humanity. As the 19th century German philosopher Georges Misch put it: "… the echo [philosophical concerns] awoke in us may just be something that the natural course of human life awakes in every human, quite spontaneously, at one time or another."[5] Thus, the following reflection on philosophy, although not from the Hellenic *poleis*, or city-states, held as much resonance for ancient Athenians as they should for readers of today:

> [The seeker of wisdom is the one] whose heart is informed about these things which would be otherwise ignored, the one who is clear-sighted when he [or she] is deep into a problem, the one who is moderate in his [or her] actions, who penetrates ancient writings, whose advice is [sought] to unravel complications, who is really wise, who instructed his [or her] own heart, who stays awake at night as he [or she] looks for the right paths, who surpasses what he [or she] accomplished yesterday, who is wiser than a sage, who brought him [or her] self to wisdom, who asks for advice and sees to it that he [or she] is asked advice. ("Inscription of Antef," 12th Dynasty, Kmt, 1991–1782 BCE)[6]

Kmt—Ancient Greek name, *Aigyptos*—is what we know today as Ancient Egypt. Kmt is also known as Kemet, but I prefer simply eliminating the vowels since that is how the word was written in hieratic and hieroglyphs. More than a millennium before the emergence of the Presocratic philosophers (6th century BCE), Antef's reflections offer no doubt about early metaphilosophical reflection. "Metaphilosophy" refers both to reflection on philosophy and philosophy of philosophy. Antef's reference to other "ancient" writings offer additional intellectual resources that, given the conceptual framework of "upper" Kmt being southward in his context, lead us into a world in which the night offered the beauty and wonder from the stars and the journey of human reflection.[7] As the architect, philosopher, and physician Imhotep, as did subsequently Hor-Djed-Ef, Kagemni, Ptahhotep, and Lady Peseshet, pondered several hundred years earlier, the night sky in Antef's time also stimulated awe and reflection, as it could for those of us today who embrace such an opportunity free of light pollution.

Though the word "philosophy" is often translated as "the love of wisdom," it represents an important meeting of languages and worlds as the Greek words *philia* and *philo* (fondness or devotional love) was conjoined with the transformed word *sophia* (wisdom), whose origin was more southern than many proponents may prefer. It is from the Mdw Ntr word *Sbyt* ("wise teachings"). The related word *Sba* ("to teach" or "to be wise") was transformed through the ancient Greek tendency to transform the Mdw Ntr "*b*" to "*ph*" or, in English, "*f*."

The path to such understanding is even more circuitous than discussion would afford here, as the problem of prejudice we are now exploring with regard to philosophy emerges as well with etymology and archaeolinguistics. Ending one's investigations repeatedly in Greek and Latin eventually leads to the false presumption—as found, for instance, in the thought of Martin Heidegger—that thinking began with the emergence of those languages (though he was not particularly kind to Latin).[8] Lost hopes of the radical difference between Africans, Asians, Europeans, Indigenous peoples of North America and South America, and the Oceania peoples at the biological level as revealed in the theory of natural selection, the commitment to radical anthropological difference moved to linguistic polygenesis, despite logic suggesting linguistic creativity and adaptation from where language had to have begun (that is, among the earliest peoples of Africa).[9]

The people of Kmt and Kush, a country among the Nubians from the south, had many nuanced ways of thinking about concepts such as knowing, learning, and wisdom, ranging from *Rkh* (to know), to *rkht* ("accurate knowledge," "science," in the sense of inquiring into the nature of things [*kht*]), and good (*nfr*) judgment (*wpt,* often transliterated as *upi*). The word *wpt/upi* means "to judge," "to discern," that is, "to dissect." (The "*w*" is pronounced "*ou*"; the "*A*" is a guttural "*ah*" and the "*a*" is more like "*ay*.") The cognate *tpsSmt* (often transliterated as *upset*) means "specify." The word *sAt* (prudential wisdom) set the stage for *sAA* (wisdom), which also refers to the wise person (*sAA*) who also seeks *sAw* (saiety) through being *sAi* (wise). To ask if this "satisfies" the reader should, through a pun, reiterate the point.

The intellectual meeting of worlds that historically met in every other respect was not new, and what should be noticed is that throughout such meetings, reflections on what such intellectual work was about immediately followed. Antef, for instance, was reflecting both on philosophy and the philosopher. Later on, in his *Symposium*, Plato (actual name Aristokles) similarly reflected on the love of wisdom and the difficulty of loving its lover—in that text's case, the young Alcibiades' love of his senior beloved Socrates. Thus, the origins of philosophy on the continent in which humanity evolved—Africa—versus the one that subsequently dominated much of the globe—Europe—are not as distant as many scholars of their subsequent intellectual histories led many, if not most, to believe. Beyond that south-to-north and west-to-east movement, there were, as well, many others in which human beings, as thinking creatures, produced ideas while migrating into every direction. Wherever human beings were afforded sufficient time for reflection, ideas on organization and the makeup of reality followed.

Philosophy, then, should be placed among the plethora of human efforts to understand our relationship to reality, which includes each other, and the subsequent professionalizing of that task into the academically formalized discipline housed in universities today. This distinction offers additional challenges since it is possible for the latter to become so focused that it ceases to offer intellectual contributions beyond the demonstration of skill. The former thus always speaks to humanity (and whatever kinds of beings that could communicate ideas), whereas the latter at times does such, though not always intentionally so.

What philosophers do is also a complicated and fluid matter. Some proponents regard their activity as a battle for truth. In that version, one "wins" through "knocking down" one's "opponents" through demonstrating the "weaknesses" of their arguments. A problem with that model is that it is possible to win arguments, become hegemonic, and yet be wrong. What makes an argument "weak" is at times a component taken to be false because of a system of presuppositions against it such as the notion of the absolute reach and completeness of the language that deems it unintelligible. And what makes one "strong" could be its formal presentation despite its clearly being false. Think of the proofs against motion and time offered by the 5th century BCE philosopher Zeno of Elea. He famously pointed out that one must cross an infinitesimal number of steps before even being able to make a complete step or achieve a whole moment in time. Acknowledging the validity of the form of his arguments, one could simply check one's watch, get up, and walk on one's way to one's appointment. Think also, for example, of the once presumed absolute reach and completeness of Euclidean geometry with its axiom of a straight line as we have now come to realize we live in a world of curved space and more. Or think of the presumed failure of languages without the copula "is." Truth, from Old English *trīewth* and *trēowth*, meaning that in which one should invest one's faith, can be preserved without stating "*x* is *y*."

Another model of philosophy holds metaphors of midwifery, communication, collaboration, collective curiosity—in short, working together to appreciate, hear, see, and understand—and at times, even discover—what we often fail to engage or comprehend. In this version, philosophy is not only a communicative practice but also a social enterprise, contrary to the Cartesian model of self-seclusion, of increasing or unleashing human intellectual potential. In this sense, philosophy is also humanity reaching beyond itself. It is no accident that many of its metaphors, from antiquity to recent times, are about the human struggle to escape prisons and caves of ignorance.

The focus of philosophy in different parts of the world over the ages varied according to the priorities of where it was practiced. Among ancient East Africans, for instance, astronomy, architecture, and medicine offered paths to philosophical reflection, and the complicated negotiation of power among increasingly dense populations of peoples occasioned much reflection on balance, justice, laws, right, and truth. In Kmt, the concept of *MAat* addressed such themes.[10] Among the Greek-speaking peoples, *dikaiosunē* was similar.[11] In East Asia, similar concerns about learning, order, rule, and respect emerged, especially in *Ruism*, most known today as Confucianism.[12]

A trend of perfecting or at least improving marked these developments and questions flowed over the ages as human beings struggled with concerns of eternity and change, appearance and reality, right and wrong, to a point of generating questions that, despite the various preferences across philosophical groups and individual philosophers, amount to familiar concerns with matters ranging from nature and the natural to the knowable and the possible. Questions about what must be, what exists, for what human beings should aspire, the meaning and possibility of freedom as well as proper, correct, or justified forms of reasoning, the reach and conditions of knowledge, the good life, whether reality has a purpose or purposes, the best organization of power, and value of all things, among many more, connect philosophers across time and cultural divides.

These questions generate various "fields" in which thinkers address them under the now specialized terms of aesthetics, axiology, epistemology, ethics, existentialism, metaphysics, ontology, philosophy of education, philosophy of mind, philosophical logic, political philosophy, and more through approaches such as analytical philosophy, phenomenology, pragmatism, and hermeneutics. Drawing upon and extending beyond these are also constellations of ideas and challenges under rubrics of philosophical anthropology, philosophy of culture, Africana or African Diasporic philosophy, decolonial philosophy, feminist philosophy, philosophy of liberation, transcendentalism, and vitalism. These are not exhaustive, but they give a sense of the fecundity of philosophical expression.

There has been and unfortunately continues to be the use of such reflections also for rationalizations and evasions of human responsibility not only to each other but also to other aspects of reality. Philosophy, thus, also historically faced, as we see from the beginning of this reflection, its own integrity. Euromodern colonialism, for instance, stimulated lines of ethnophilosophical movements often disguised as "universal" and "primary." Thus, Anglophone empiricism and European continental rationalism paved paths to what are today known as Anglo-analytical philosophy and (European) continental philosophy. African and Asian philosophies orient themselves in professional philosophy in relation to these, and First Nations and Indigenous peoples of many kinds among colonized countries stand in relation to these hegemonic organizations of philosophical identity. Euromodern philosophy, in other words, exemplified a form of epistemic colonialism or, as the Peruvian social theorist Aníbal Quijano formulated it, drawing upon ideas from World Systems and Dependency Theory, *coloniality*.[13]

Additionally, Euromodern interpretations of the history of philosophy have led to a false presupposition of neat divides between religious and theological thought on the one hand and secular naturalistic philosophy on the other. Despite disavowals of conceptual and normative commitments from Jewish, Christian, and Islamic resources, many normative presuppositions of these "world religions" could be found in so-called Western philosophical thought as those of other traditions such as Akan or Yorùbá in Africa or Hinduism, Buddhism, and Daoism in Asia or Aztec or Mayan in Central America.[14]

Last, but not exhaustively, universality and primary or first questions made epistemology take the historic stage as first philosophy in Euromodern thought. Much of what is called Anglo-analytical philosophy and Eurocontinental philosophy rest on this presupposition, though there has been no shortage, from Friedrich Nietzsche to Edmund Husserl to Michel Foucault and

Richard Rorty, of internal critics. A crucial point of convergence is that while debates emerged over whether epistemology, ethics, or metaphysics should stand as first or *fundamental* philosophy, the people whose humanity was challenged in Euromodernity were not afforded the luxury of thinking through which one was ultimately prevalent—since, as many learned, each philosophical road led to another. Instead, a historic question of humanity came to the fore: in an age of challenged membership in the human world, philosophical anthropology proved inevitable.

We come, then, to philosophical questions of "application" and endemic concerns. The former simply applies philosophical presuppositions to the study of Africans, the African Diaspora, and peoples of the Global South. The latter questions the applicability of such presuppositions. The first presumes the universality of Euromodern philosophy. The second raises concerns of metaphilosophical critique; it places philosophy, in any form, under critical scrutiny.[15]

Today most Africans, or at least what most people mean when they call people "African," are also black people, and the history of ideas and science offers no short supply of scandalous rationalizations of human degradation in their regard and many other nonwhite peoples'.[16] History has also shown that black people, as philosophers and social scientists from the Haitian anthropologist, jurist, philosopher, and statesman Anténor Firmin to the African American economist, historian, philosopher, and sociologist W.E.B. Du Bois and many others have argued, do not always fit into many disciplinary norms except as "problems."[17] In short, their "fit" is paradoxically one of not fitting. A theodicean form of reasoning about application follows, where discipline is presumed to be godlike and thus intrinsically complete and valid, which means the failure of some people to fit or, perhaps more accurately, "behave" is an expression of their iniquity and infelicity. Something "must be," in a word, "wrong" with such people.

Du Bois observed doubled levels of experience and research in such circumstances. Phenomenologically, there is double consciousness—the realization of how black people are perceived and the lived-reality of black consciousness. Where the system of knowledge, the philosophical presuppositions, is questioned, a movement of realized contradictions results in a dialectical unleashing of knowledge. This dialectical movement, of examining the contradictions inherent in *making people into problems at epistemological, sociological, and political levels*, is a core insight of the kind of philosophy that took a path from black philosophy to Africana philosophy.

This kind of philosophy takes three fundamental questions posed by black people's relation to Euromodernity seriously: (1) What does it mean to be human? (2) What is freedom? and (3) How are justificatory practices justifiable in light of the historic and continued challenges to reason posed by colonialism, enslavement, racism, and cultivated dependency not only as material and political projects but also intellectual enterprises? The third question stimulated a unique branch of inquiry, as it raised the question of whether material impositions entail epistemic ones. Put differently, what could be done of reason when colonialism produced colonial forms? This led to a crisis of reason. Working backward, each question is symbiotically linked to the other, for dehumanization presupposes humanization; fighting against enslavement demands freedom; and the kinds of reasoning involved in all three, including offering a critique of reason itself, brings them together.

Africana philosophy has a rich history of debates on the questions of being human, free, and reasoning outlined here. The Martinican revolutionary psychiatrist and philosopher Frantz Fanon was among those who formulated the philosophical plight for Black philosophers (capitalized because thinking for him was a matter of agency and committed struggle, which transformed racial objects from "blacks" into human subjects—"Blacks"): where even reason is made unreasonable, the challenge for African philosophers (and by extension all in the African Diaspora and those designated "black") is to reason with unreasonable reason *reasonably*.[18] This strange formulation brings to the fore ironically a relationship with philosophy beyond Euromodernity in a connection with the ancient Antef and, as well, to descendants whom none of us today will ever know.

This concluding reflection brings forth an additional element of philosophical concern. The movements from double consciousness to a dialectical relationship with the Euromodern world pose the following. Euromodernity produced a special form of alienation through the transformation of whole groups of people into categories of "indigenous"/"native," "enslaved," "colonized," and "black." Such people suffer a unique form of melancholia (bereavement from loss or separation), as they are indigenous to a world that rejects them by virtue of making them into problems. Their "home," by virtue of such identities, is, unfortunately, a homeless one. A critic may ask about what this means specifically for "the" African, who, like the First Nations of North America, South America, and Oceania, in her own home, "belongs." For her, looking at Africa is much like its etymological origins of looking to the opening of the *Ka* ("the womb" and "life," whose connection to the subsequent Hebrew word *chai*, and perhaps the Chinese word *chi/ki/qi*, should by now be apparent). On that matter, we need simply to admit the *globality* of the Euromodern age. The homelessness of which I speak is not geographic. It is temporal, even where one is geographically in one's home. The African, in other words, struggles paradoxically, as do the African Diaspora, with being temporally homeless at home.

The realization of that problem as a function of Euromodernity is also a form of transcending it, which entails two considerations. The first is that the particularizing of Euromodernity raises the question of other *Modernities*. The question of what it means to be modern shifts, then, to a question of time and the future. "Primitive," after all, means belonging to the past (from *primitus*, "at first" or "earlier"). Once posed as having a future, Africana philosophical reflection becomes an expression of Afromodernity. This means the possibility of agency in history and responsibility for a future whose specificities are open. The struggle with reason becomes a form of reason beyond reason as presently conceived, and, in turn, it leads to metaphilosophical reflection of Africana philosophy as the paradox of philosophy being willing to transcend itself. This effort is a call for the decolonization of philosophy, which requires a rejection of philosophical parochialism (false claims of universality) and a demand for ongoing, universalizing philosophical practices in which ideas connect across disciplines, fields, and peoples without collapsing into delusions of completeness and the idolatry of divine embodiment.

Philosophy, understood in this way, is also, then, despite protest throughout the ages, an expression, among others, of humanity's search, at the level of ideas about our relationship with reality—which, as we will see, is greater than ontological dictates—for a home to which one does not return but instead for which one searches and, along the way, through its decolonization, builds.

Notes

1. For discussion of creolization and mixedness, especially in methodological terms, as I am using them here, see Jane Anna Gordon, *Creolizing Political Theory: Reading Rousseau through Fanon* (New York, NY: Fordham University Press, 2014).
2. For analysis, see Charles Finch, *Nile Genesis: An Introduction to the Opus of Gerald Massey* (2006), 8. Available on line (2006): https://minorvictorianwriters.org.uk/massey/cmc_nile_genesis.htm.
3. In this sense, one could argue that psychoanalytical reflection is primordial wherever there is the realization of existence, which is, paradoxically, a transcending of being or permanence. I will return to this reflection, but with regard to this observation speaking volumes, see, more recently, Barnaby B. Barratt's *What Is Psychoanalysis?: 100 Years after Freud's "Secret Committee"* (London, UK: Routledge, 2013), *Radical Psychoanalysis: An Essay on Free-Associate Praxis* (London, UK: Routledge, 2016), and *Beyond Psychotherapy: On Becoming a (Radical) Psychoanalyst* (London, UK: Routledge, 2019).
4. Critical sources are many. See, for example, Peter J. K. Park, *Africa, Asia, and the History of Philosophy Racism in the Formation of the Philosophical Canon, 1780–1830* (Albany, NY: SUNY Press, 2013), Kwasi Wiredu (ed.), *A Companion to African Philosophy* (Malden, MA: Blackwell Publishers, 2004), and P.H. Coetzee and A.P.J. Rous (eds.), *The African Philosophy Reader: A Text with Readings*, 2nd Edition (London, UK: Routledge, 2003). For a recent example of the Greek "miracle" paradigm, see Eric Weiner, *The Geography of Genius: Lessons from the World's Most Creative Places*, Reprint Edition (New York, NY: Simon and Schuster, 2016).
5. See, for example, George Misch, *The Dawn of Philosophy: A Philosophy Primer* (Cambridge, MA: Harvard University Press, 1951), 25.
6. "Inscription of Antef," 12th Dynasty, Kmt/Ancient Egypt, 1991–1782 BCE. I amended the translation because Antef was not referring exclusively to male philosophers. This well-known inscription (among Egyptologists) is discussed by Théophile Obeng in his "Egypt: Ancient History of African Philosophy," in Wiredu (ed.), *A Companion to African Philosophy*, 35. See also Obenga's *La Philosophie africaine de la période pharaonique: 2780–330 avant notre ère* (Paris, France: L'Harmattan, 1990) and Molefe Kete Asante, *The Egyptian Philosophers: Ancient African Voices from Imhotep*

to Akhenaten (Chicago, IL: African American Images, 2000). For original, see Heinrich Brugsch (ed.), *Thesaurus Inscriptionum Aegyptiacarum: Woerterbuch Suppl.*, 6 vols. (Leipsig, Germany: Graz, 1883–1891).

7. For some of those ancient sources see, *Writings from Ancient Egypt*, trans. Toby Wilkinson (London, UK: Penguin Classics, 2016). See especially the anonymous "Be a Writer," where the author lists, among earlier writers, Imhotep, Nefertiti or Khety, Ptahemdjehuty, Khakheperraseneb, Ptahhotep, and Kairsu, 287.

8. Elaboration of Heidegger's intellectual chauvinism and racism will take us too far afield. For discussion, see Eric Nelson, *Chinese and Buddhist Philosophy in Early Twentieth-Century German Thought* (London, UK: Bloomsbury Academic, 2017). Heidegger and his followers, for instance, treated reflections on Being and beings— that is, ontology—as though failure to do so was to fall short of actually doing philosophy. For exploration of other metaphilosophical fallacies along the ideas offered here, see Lewis R. Gordon, *Disciplinary Decadence: Living Thought in Trying Times* (New York, NY: Routledge, 2006) and "Decolonizing Philosophy," *The Southern Journal of Philosophy* 57, Spindel Supplement (2019): 16–36. See also Keiji Nishitani, *Religion and Nothingness*, trans. Jan Van Bragt (Berkeley, CA: University of California Press, 1982) for a critique of much of Western philosophy, including Heidegger, as failing to understand how beings and Being cover over reality, which would make ontology-centrism ultimately a fetish.

9. See Cheikh Anta Diop's *Parenté Génétique de L'Égyptien Pharaonique et des Langues Negro-Africaines* (Ifan-Dakar: Nouvelles Éditions Africaines, 1977) and *Cheikh Anta Diop: L'homme et l'oeuvres* (Paris: Présence Africaine, 2003), Charles Finch, III, *Echoes of the Old Darkland: Themes from the African Eden* (Decatur, GA: Khenti, Inc., 1977) and Gerald Massey, *The Natural Genesis* (Baltimore, MD: Black Classics Press, 1998 [1883]).

10. Sources are numerous. In addition to the ancient references offered thus far, see also *The Eloquent Peasant*, 2nd Edition, trans. Loren R. Fischer (Eugene, OR: Cascade, 2015). Composed in approximately 1850 BCE, this tale is also a meditation on *MAat*, often translated as "justice" but actually meaning much more, from the perspective of a protagonist at the lower wrung of Kmt society. I return to this concept in Chapter 3.

11. This term is also often translated as "justice" but, in fact, means more. I return to this concept in Chapter 3, but for an excellent summary of the limitations of translating this term as justice, see Alisdair MacIntyre, *After Virtue*, 3rd Edition (South Bend, IN: Notre Dame University Press, 2007), especially 134.

12. On the errors of referring to Ruism as Confucianism, see, for example, Bin Song, "A Catechism of Confucianism: Is Confucius a Confucian?" *HuffPost* (February 9, 2016; updated December 6, 2017): https://www.huffpost.com/entry/a-catechism-of-confuciani_6_b_9178068. Think also, in this tradition, of dynamic harmony (*he*, 和), which is related to *MAat* and *dikaiosuné* but not identical with them, and often translated into English as "peace." For additional discussion, see also Eric Nelson, *Chinese and Buddhist Philosophy in Early Twentieth-Century German Thought* and *Alexus McLeod, Understanding Asian Philosophy: Ethics in the Analects, Zhuangzi, Dhammapada, and Bhagavad Gita* (London, UK: Bloomsbury, 2014).

13. Aníbal Quijano, "Modernity, Identity, and Utopia in Latin America," in Michael Arona, John Beverly, and José Oviedo (eds.), *The Postmodernism Debate in Latin America* (Durham: Duke University Press, 1995), 201–216, and "Coloniality of Power, Eurocentrism, and Latin America," *Nepantla: Views from South* 1, no. 3 (2000): 533–580.

14. For critique of the notion of the "West," see K. Anthony Appiah, "There Is No Such Thing as Western Civilization," *The Guardian* (9 November 2016): https://www.theguardian.com/world/2016/nov/09/western-civilisation-appiah-reith-lecture?CMP=share_btn_fb. In addition to the sources on African philosophy

cited thus far, also see Kwame Gyekye, *An Essay on African Philosophical Thought: The Akan Conceptual Scheme*, Revised Edition (Philadelphia, PA: Temple University Press, 1997), Nkiru Nzegwu, *Family Matters: Feminist Concepts in African Philosophy of Culture* (Albany, NY: State University of New York Press, 2006), and Alena Rettová, *Afrophone Philosophies: Reality and Challenge* (Cologne, Germany: Rüdiger Köppe Verlag 2007); and, for Aztec and Mayan philosophy, see James Maffie, *Aztec Philosophy: Understanding a World in Motion* (Boulder, CO: University of Colorado Press, 2015), and Alexus McLeod, *Philosophy of the Ancient Maya: Lords of Time* (Lanham, MD: Lexington Books, 2017).

15. For elaboration, see Lewis R. Gordon, *An Introduction to Africana Philosophy*, 2nd Edition (Cambridge, MA: Cambridge University Press, 2008).

16. Studies are many, but see especially Stephen Jay Gould, *The Mismeasure of Man*, revised and expanded edition (New York, NY: W.W. Norton, 1996) and Angela Saini, *Superior: The Return of Race Science* (Noida, India: HarperCollins Publishers India, 2019). For an anthology with excerpts from primary sources, see also see Robert Bernasconi and Tommy Lott (eds.), *The Idea of Race* (Indianapolis, IN: Hackett Publishers, 2000).

17. See, for example, Anténor Firmin, *Equality of Human Races: A Nineteenth Century Haitian Scholar's Response to European Racialism*, trans. Asselin Charles (New York, NY: Garland Publishers, 2000 [1885]) and W.E.B. Du Bois, *The Souls of Black Folk: Essays and Sketches* (Chicago, IL: A.C. McClurg & Co., 1903). For discussion, also see Lewis R. Gordon, *An Introduction to Africana Philosophy* and *Existentia Africana: Understanding Africana Existential Thought* (New York, NY: Routledge, 2000), Chapter 4, and Jane Anna Gordon, "The Gift of Double Consciousness: Some Obstacles to Grasping the Contributions of the Colonized," in Nalini Persram (ed.), *Postcolonialism and Political Theory* (Lanham, MD: Lexington Books, 2007), 143–161.

18. I elaborate on Fanon's observation in Lewis R. Gordon, *What Fanon Said: A Philosophical Introduction to His Life and Thought* (New York, NY: Fordham UP; London, UK: Hurst; Johannesburg, South Africa: Wits University Press, 2015). Fanon made this observation in the fifth chapter of his classic inaugural book *Peau noire, masques blancs* (Paris, France: Éditions du Seuil, 1952), known in English as *Black Skin, White Masks*, trans. Charles Lamm Markmann (New York, NY: Grove Press, 1967) and the recent translation by Richard Philcox for Grove in 2008.

Chapter 2

Re-Imagining Liberations

"Diversity" has become a mantra that, without the proviso of critique, could collapse into familiar and paradoxical tropes of celebrating diversity without a difference, or, specifically, power difference. In the United States, for example, diversity is publicly praised while, in practice, it often stops short of structural access to those who are black, brown, or indigenous.

I begin with such reflection because the thoughts that follow were organized from a public lecture I presented at the 2018 Centre for Diversity Studies International Conference at the University of Witwatersrand in Johannesburg, South Africa. That meeting was devoted to "(re)imagining liberations."[1]

There are many academic, civic, and even private corporate institutions across the globe celebrating diversity so long as the celebrants avow an allergy to liberation. It is difficult, after all, to talk about liberation without paying attention to the mechanisms of invasion, colonization, enslavement, genocide, and ongoing degradation of human life on which liberal democracies are built in the Euromodern age. This is not to say that liberation was not a prior concern. If the Seder ceremony conducted by Jews during *Pesach* (Passover) is any indication, thinking about liberation is a tradition that has gone on for a long time, even for people whose relationship to it has now become one of ambivalence. For Afro-Jews, for instance, this reflection on liberation is more recent, as not only the liberation struggles of former colonies of Europe attest but also the ongoing realities of continued enslavement and practices of colonialism under other names.[2]

The contemporary global situation is one in which "liberation" is a question at the heart of the intellectual and political condition of the Global South. For the North, marked by the logic of having—indeed, *having it all*—there is nothing from which to be liberated or toward which radical transformation of society should be sought except, perversely, liberation *from liberation*. The aims are to make the course of historical, dehumanizing developments more rigorous, which are already underway. Beyond that, there is, seemingly, only the zero-sum logic of things to lose. There is, then, relative fluidity of North and South, where the call for liberation includes Southern sites even in the geographical North and resistance to it is a feature of geopolitical Northern outposts in the geographical South. Such is the folly.

The immediate difference, then, is about the fundamental core organization of contemporary global life. If that foundation is fundamentally flawed, then the demand to fix it follows. If presumed intrinsically sound, efforts of transformation would be conceived of as nothing short of the advancement of injustice.[3]

Thinking Otherwise, Decolonial Considerations, and Beyond

Is it possible to think—and by extension *do*—otherwise? Much depends on the resources of thinking at hand and those we—and by "we" I mean those of us committed to things changing—build. The inherited legacy is straightforward. Euromodern capitalism, colonialism, enslavement, racism, and sexism produced a world whose legacy is one in which legitimate thinking and acting are exemplified by its beneficiaries. The specific history boils down to people who are designated white and, preferably, very affluent. Even where not primarily marked by financial wealth, whiteness in many places functions as an enormous asset.[4] For the rest, a multitude of problems arise.

One is a dualism of legitimate and illegitimate study distinguished by the logic of belonging and not belonging in Euromodern societies. Consider the example of race. An often unsaid presumption is that those who are designated white think and research and those who are designated brown and black must be "taught" or rely on "experience."[5] It is a position that is historically applied to the categories "man" and "woman," as well, but as these are ultimately fluid, relational terms, they often, except where specified otherwise, presume white signification against which are posed "racialized man" and "racialized woman." This is mapped onto institutions and the resources they receive. We could call this *epistemic dependency*. It is most known today as *epistemic colonization*.

Why is this a form of colonization and dependency? Although experience at first may seem emancipatory—after all, one's experience is one's *own*—the problem of experience is that it often requires clarification and interpretation. Everyone has had the experience, in other words, of trying to figure out her experience. The ordinary response is to seek advice, converse with another, and bring a theory to that experience through which it could gain an interpretation and become meaningful. If the only interpreters and theorists sought are white—which is for the most part the practice of looking to European thinkers whenever concerns of theory arise—the result would be an affirmation of thinking and theorizing as white.

The problem goes further. If those white thinkers and theorists developed their thought through drawing upon their experience, then appealing to their thought as the primary basis of interpretation would make their experiences also more legitimate than people who are not white. There would, thus, be a double degradation of the value of colonized life. It is not only colonized people's thought that would be denied or devalued but also their experience.

What makes this ironic for people of color is that the outcome is from an effort to legitimize their experience. Legitimizing their experience through the thought and experiences of those who reject it is an act of delegitimizing their experience. It would make even the colonizers' experience superior.

This thought exercise raises one of the conundrums of what is known today as decolonization and decoloniality.[6] On the one hand, there is the intrinsic "violence" of decolonization. It involves, as Frantz Fanon observed in *Les damnés de la terre*, which I will from here onward refer to as *The Damned of the Earth*, replacing former colonial governors.[7] This replacement could also be epistemic. Replacement, however, is not intrinsically liberatory or revolutionary. In prosaic language, that would involve changing the players but not the game. The proverbial game involves practices through which games are made at all. This is what led some critics of colonization to think about dependency and, thus, use the term "coloniality," whose antithesis, they argue, is "decoloniality."[8] This involves the mechanisms of reason through which imposed dependency is produced. I add "imposed" since self-cultivated dependency— such as obsessive love—is paradoxical in that it involves desires of conquest, invasion, and possession leading to being, in effect, possessed by the objects of such investments, even where such "objects" have no interest in doing so.[9] There are also forms of dependency outside of the framework of social production or desire, such as birds', insects', and mammals' need for oxygen.

There is a geographical conception already marked in concepts such as North and South. It is a hierarchy in which North represents "up" and South represents "down" or "below." Yet as below is a relational term that makes sense only from a perspective of what is designated above, it is not fixed and can, thus, pop up nearly anywhere or at any time. Researchers of ancient cartography often discover, for instance, that to render many regions of the Mediterranean recognizable, they have to turn ancient maps upside down. Because of this fundamental relativity of all hierarchical relations, there is a symbiotic relationship that follows in which a reproduced dependency at times emerges ironically through the project of decoloniality. As we saw with experience, the project of its legitimation could lead to its delegitimation, so, too, with coloniality, which, when placed as a prime objective, may "need" coloniality for its continued legitimacy.

An intellectually specific articulation of this is easily seen in the relationship of decoloniality to poststructuralism. This movement in European thought affected discussions of theory throughout the Euromodern academy across the globe from the late 1960s through to the early 2000s. Many saw it as a liberatory development in thought. Although there were many varieties, three dominant ones were archaeological, genealogical, and textual poststructuralisms. All are avowed forms of antiessentialism. The first involved tracing through conditions from which various orders of knowledge arose. The second disclosed manifestations of power in various forms of knowledge or values. And the third, of which Jacque Derrida's Deconstruction was the most famous exemplar, examined moments of textual undecidability, including efforts to appeal to meaning beyond texts. A crisis emerged in these areas of thought at both empirical and conceptual levels. At the empirical level, the popularity of these ways of thinking during the growth and eventual hegemony of neoliberalism and new resources of colonization created doubt about the incompatibility of poststructuralism with such politically undermining developments. At the conceptual level, critics increasingly identified essentialism in those forms of antiessentialism. As major exemplars of theory in competition with philosophy—the discipline that once built temples of thought—poststructuralism for the most part was not able to produce viable responses to these challenges.[10] Failing such, its practitioners resorted to the age-old technique of rebranding themselves. Poststructuralism continues as of the writing of this reflection under the nomenclatures of critical theory (which is primarily textual and sometimes genealogical) and decoloniality (which is primarily genealogical).

This observation of decoloniality—we could say "decolonialism," but that would be unacceptable to the practitioners—suggests that postructuralism functions within decoloniality as a colonial element or form of coloniality. If this is so, that would be an additional crisis for poststructuralism. For decoloniality, this problem becomes acute where theory is undertheorized. Where this is so, the result is often an appeal to theorists with the addition of a *position* on an issue. That position—often formulated as "positionality"—is often a moral one offered as a political intervention. This development is not unique to decolonial thought, as we shall see. What it raises is a consideration beyond decoloniality, which is the question of the scope and impact of impediments to proffered thought.

Shifting the Geography and Practice of Reason

Returning to the problem of privileged geopolitical locations of thought, it does not follow from these critical reflections that there is no alternative to colonized or subjugated forms of thinking or reasoning. If reason is asserted as a specific, geopolitical location, the emergence of another site of reason could create a seismic shift. This could occur as a delegitimation of the initially posed reason as, paradoxically, unreasonable. Or it could occur through particularizing that reason as one among others. If the initial manifestation of reason can only sustain itself as reason-in-and-of-itself, then the mere idea of different kinds of reason would defang its hegemony.

There is another consideration. One could create a shift in the geography of reason through teleologically suspending it. By teleological suspension, I mean the paradox of being willing to go beyond the initially stated reason *for the sake of reason.* In plain language, it means to take on the task of building alternatives without worry of recognition from former governors or embodiments of avowed reason. As reason could go beyond itself for the sake of reason, decoloniality could be similar. Decolonial thinkers must, from this point of view, go beyond decoloniality for the sake of decoloniality. The decolonial theorist Catherine Walsh articulates this consideration as "decoloniality *for.*"[11] She, in effect, argues for shifting the geography of legitimacy in which reason could only come *from* colonial models of power and thought. In one sense, she exemplifies a rearticulated genealogical poststructuralist claim. In another—given the implicit teleology "for" though not in the dreaded grand narrative form—she transcends it.

This consideration of self-transcending decoloniality raises an important problem of what follows when decoloniality becomes an objective instead of a means. Without thinking about what decoloniality is for, it becomes a fetish and collapses into familiar patterns of religiosity, idolatry, and its accompanying moralistic investments. For instance, fetishism and moralism appeal to models of purity. This means, in effect, elimination of all that is not consistent with preferred or avowed systems or those who embody them. The effect is a form of puritanism that makes purification into a moral ideal. This aim of decolonization *from* leads to no one ever being decolonized enough except, perhaps, the one who poses the problem of decolonization, with decoloniality being its purest commitment. That person faces the possibility of not having been decolonized, which raises the problem of the *source* of decolonial problems. This inward search turns away from political conditions of political problems—because politics is too messy to serve as pure criteria—and moves toward a quest for the moral subordination of political life. That this resulting moralism is compatible with neoliberalism, which privileges the moral individual over political subjects, in effect leaves structural inequalities intact.

Take, for example, moralistic discussions of racism. The focus on "privilege" and decolonizing the self of such often takes the form of moral self-repudiation. Eventually, anything one has that another person lacks becomes a privilege without questioning whether what is possessed is something that others should have. When rights to resources such as clean water, food, education, public safety, and justice become "privileges," what is a reasonable person supposed to do? Should she give those up?

The unfortunate response is often an effusion of guilt, through which the "unprivileged" to whom it is devoted experiences the affective sense of power in the form of moral superiority. Afterward, both the privileged and the deprived return to their relative unequal material conditions in a society that remains structurally intact, when a proper response should instead be to make access to such resources universal.[12] Proponents of neoliberalism prefer—in fact, proffer and even relish—the critique of privilege model, since it would push such resources out of the realm of rights and, thus, opens the door to expanding their dissolution into the more familiar form of deprivation. Hidden in this display is a basic truth: political problems require political, not moralistic, solutions.

One may object that moral solutions can also be political ones, but this belies the basic point of liberal, neoliberal, and neoconservative thought, whose legitimate responses are ultimately moral ones.[13] The question of political responsibility only makes sense in such frameworks through "responsibility" only being a moral demand. I do not offer a detailed discussion of this distinction here since that would take us too far afield. For now, I encourage the reader to consult writings by Karl Jaspers, Steve Bantu Biko, Iris Marion Young, and some of my writings on the subject of the independence of political responsibility, where the peculiarity of responsibility in political terms transcends the scope of morality.[14] Normative life is more than matters of good and bad, right and wrong, justice and injustice; those who bear the weight of what is to be done in such instances may transcend the scope of the divine, the legal, and the moral. Being accountable to the political means being so to what is to come, even though one may not be able to demonstrate a direct causal and epistemological understanding of what will emerge.

Shifting the geography of reason thus also requires shifting our understanding, imagination, and practices thereof.[15] It requires being willing to take leaps of thought across what are, at first thought, unthinkable. This has always been an urgent task since human history—indeed human evolution—is a story of addressing crises. Today, as global turns to the right are reassertions of force against thought, that element of our condition continues. Many across the globe are being pressured not to think imaginatively on the grounds that all could be thought have been done. It is a peculiarly Northern intellectual disease premised on all such thought having been produced or refined by Europeans and their diaspora reformulated under the moniker of "the West."[16] This would make the Euromodern world the end of history, as a rash of Eurocentric thinkers announced over the past half-century. Yet, all this, as with experience and reason, stumbles when the question is posed— end of history *for whom?* The inability of many, if not most, Euromodern subjects to think otherwise does not entail alternatives cannot be built and, in so doing, thought.

Allegorizing Allegory

It is no accident that when thought faces constraints, it often seeks refuge in what at first may not appear as such. This is the stuff of allegory. Taken literally, allegory means to speak openly about something else. It is a term that comes from putting together the Greek words *allos* ("another," "something else," and, at times, "beyond") and *agoreuein* ("to speak openly"). There is to some extent a sense in which all real thinking is allegorical. It introduces us to something that takes us out of one prison or another. Some are brilliant, as in Plato's famous allegory of the cave from his *Republic* (514a–520a), which is, in effect, an allegory about allegory. Plato asked us, through the mouth of Socrates, to imagine being taken outside of a closed environment to discover that there is a world beyond the cave. This discovery of something else that reveals the outside raises the question of the outside status of outside. Plato imagined that this movement was a unique privilege of philosophy and thus the philosopher. And its effects through today remain in those who conflate philosophy only with its forms that emerge from the northern side of the Mediterranean and Europeans' claim to its legacy. The defense is often an appeal to the etymology of the word "philosophy" as Greek, even though, as we have seen, its history reveals a meeting of linguistic resources of two continents. Recall "Sophia," often translated as "wisdom," has its origin in the African Mdw Ntr word "*sbyt*" ("wise teachings"). The related word *Sba* ("to teach" or "to be wise") was transformed through the Greek tendency to transform the Mdw Ntr "*b*" to "*ph*" or, in English, "*f*" (though the actual Greek "*ø*" has a harsh pronunciation). We should recall as well that the more ancient African language had many words built up from the root "*sa*" from which *s(a)byt* was formed. There are other words with additional roots such as "*rekh*" (also written as *rx*) as in "*rekhet*" (sometimes written as *rxt*— roughly close to awareness, intuition, knowledge of the nature of things, wise one) from which we also have English words today such as "reckon" and also the Latin word "*rex*" (which was derived from the infinitive *regere*, "to keep straight, guide, lead, or rule"). We hope an executive legislature, which is what such monarchs signified by "*rex*" mean, has the power of *rekhet*. The search into ancient sources illuminates another consideration if we bear in mind that the people of Kmt used the word *rekhet* also to mean "female knower."[17] The hieroglyph for *rekh* was of the mouth, placenta, and a rolled-up, tied, and sealed papyrus—all female signifiers. Thus, its subsequent link to "kings" is a function of the gender presuppositions of the Roman societal transformation of Kmt antiquity. The power of knowledge, at least for the latter, was not necessarily male.

I make this archaeolinguistic detour to iterate a basic point: part of the practice of epistemic colonization is to repeat the ritual of all thinking leading back to Europe. Etymology here functions, then, not simply as a methodological tool but also as an allegory. The story of philosophy is one in which *philia* (Greek) offered its devotion to *Sophia* (a transformed Mdw Ntr term). For our purposes, the presupposition of a unilateral Northern "miracle" of thought, as philosophy is often described among Euromoderns, fails because of its already creolized or mixed origins of South in the North, even though critical thinking and devotion to wisdom preceded the Athenian upsurge in recorded history by at least a few thousand years, as we saw in the "Inscription of Antef."[18] As philosophy is often claimed to be about 2,500 years old and beginning on the European continent, a clearly philosophical text written among others about 4,500 years ago on the African continent reveals the history of the now hegemonic epistemological emperors having no clothes except in the eyes of those who continue to believe in invisible cloth.

This point about origins should not be taken as simply the replacement of one beginning for another. Being first does not always mean being better, but we should bear in mind that the usefulness of the idea over thousands of years—Antef, after all, spoke of *ancient* lovers of wisdom even in his time—receives its importance from its ongoing use than its particular exemplars. Ancients of the Attic peninsula had no problem with drawing intellectual sustenance from Africa, which belies the Euromodern ideological commitment of distance between people of Southern Europe and Northeastern Africa. Instead of belaboring this point, let us just recall that as polygenic accounts of human origins lost their legitimacy, racist commitments moved into cultural and linguistic apartheid in the evolution of Euromodern thought.

White Privilege, Concealed License

This story of influence and movements of thought revealing the absence of a "pure" manifestation of ideas raises the problem of how concepts could be misrepresented in ways that mobilize erasure or at least the invisibility of many human communities' roles in the production of human phenomena. We could call this the hiding or obscuring of human agency in human institutions. In addition to academic disciplines and the places and people that produce them, there are also those institutions by which others are produced. Take, for instance, economics. Although markets are human-produced relationships going back at least a hundred thousand years—as not only did early human beings trade with each other but they also perhaps did so with other species of hominins—a conception of "*the* Market" developed in Euromodernity in England in the late 1600s.[19] Although there were many Modernities, Euromodernity emerged in the late 15th century through conflicts with Islam in which Christendom took to the Atlantic Ocean and inaugurated a historical system of global invasion and trade in which quests for profit made human beings an inconvenient necessity. The logic of the Market over markets demanded an abstraction with its own subject to replace the human ones of prior markets saturated with human sociality. The result was capitalism with its model of the rational being as a selfish creature seeking its own interests premised upon efficient and certain acquisition. Consistently applied, the conclusion of this form of subjectivity became a subject (the Market) that must, as its purpose, gobble up everything, and whose subjects (capitalists) are those who must have and do the same. The secularizing of Christendom into Europe made this subject European, and its secularized anthropology racialized non-Europeans into those who didn't belong by virtue of not having a right to anything on the basis of those who, in a form of Providence, supposedly acquired a license to everything. Although those seafaring Christians (with at times Jews and Muslims in tow) were in today's language "multiracial," their theology of purity and quest for profit eventually became rigid and acquired concrete form in a new kind of human being—namely, whites.

The logic of whiteness here is an identity that extends beyond the realm of privilege. It demands a *license*. This involves the ability to do whatever one pleases to whomever one pleases and to have whatever one wants. In short, it is the logic of a group designated under a particular system—in this case, Euromodern capitalism—to be entitled to *everything*. This entitlement extends not only to material and social resources but also to their conditions of legitimacy. Thus, in a society that substitutes moral subjects for political ones, as we find under liberalism and neoliberalism, this means possessing both sides of the equation of moral redemption. Whiteness in this sense claims not only superiority in history as those who bring morality to it but also those who historically suffer ultimately as its victims.[20]

Thus, the earlier critique of privilege discourse comes to the fore. As one cannot change one's identity willy-nilly, one gains from an outpour of guilt about the privilege of eating one's cake and having it, too—receiving the material benefits of privilege while being a victim of receiving it. A license is a different story. Although one could have the privilege of helping others, teaching, and receiving a duly deserved prize, one never has the privilege to murder, pillage, and rape. Yet, there are people throughout history who have been granted a license for such activities. Sometimes they were called "soldiers" during times of war. In practice, given the systemic protection of whites who have conducted such activities as lynching, pillaging, rape, and many other technologies of violence and theft against non-whites or those they deemed not white enough, the status of whiteness is historically a license. Think of the radical implication of license exemplified in the infamous formulation "license to kill." It means being able to kill with impunity. On the one hand, we could reflect on then candidate for presidency of the United States Donald Trump's remark that he could shoot someone to death in mid-town Manhattan, NYC, without suffering any negative consequence. This was also a statement to white supremacists who longed for their "good old days" or "the way things used to be." On the other, we need simply to look at the many historical photographs of white settlers across the world who posed without reservation in front of their butchered human prizes at lynchings and pogroms. Should anyone ever have such a license? Should anyone continue to maintain it?

Here we have questions about which people can actually do something. One can actively fight against a license on the grounds that no one should ever have what it permits. To reject things that one can fight for every human being to have is a different matter. Thus, even if one were designated the identity of a historically problematic group, one could realistically fight against a license available to that group on the grounds that no one should have such. This struggle moves from a moral conviction into the realm of political action.

Politics Unveiled

This, of course, raises the question of what it means to act politically. Continuing our allegorical use of archaeolinguistics, a clue is already in the word. From the ancient Greek word *pólis* (roughly translated as city-state) and *politeia* (roughly, citizenship or living a political life), the study of *politika* (activities or affairs of the city-state), the idea is linked to activities of citizenship. Many people confuse cities with urban structures and the notion of them existing before citizens. Since it takes people to build both, it should be clear that it is citizenship that creates cities, and cities—places of citizenship—need not be the urban environments we think of today such as Beijing, Chicago, Delhi, Johannesburg, London, Mexico City, Nairobi, New York, Paris, Sydney, or Tokyo. In fact, it could easily be shown that there are urban centers called cities today that are actually drained of citizenship. They have become, like Disneyworld, urban structures of entertainment and employment designed for that purpose. Citizenship as human communities organized for the cultivation of what turns out to be uniquely human activities and their sustainability is, of course, much older than its Greek-speaking instantiations by thousands of years, as attested to by Damascus, Gaza, Mn Nfr, Ur, Urk, and Waset. In Greek antiquity, which influenced much subsequent political thought because of the empires it inspired, one who abdicates citizenship or political activity was an *idiōtēs*. For them, that means foregoing public life for the private in which one's speech also disappears because one is no longer heard. Speech is a crucial feature of citizenship. It is what facilitates social appearance and also enables conflict without war. The word *idiōtēs* is linked to the Mdw Ntr word *idi*, which means "deaf." The whole point was that in societies in which politics is conducted live, in-person—that is, in the flesh and through speech—to hear and to be heard were crucial.

Politics involves the power of speech in the production of power through which human beings are able to govern their existence. Notice the distinction here between politics and governing. Government, properly understood, is supposed to be a tool of politics. In this sense, the government achieves its legitimacy from politics, which makes sovereignty not located in government but instead in the authority brought to it. Here, we find a distinction between "authority" and "authoritative." A government could be an authority without being authoritative. In such instances, it has lost its legitimacy and, thus, relies purely on force. Where it is authoritative, the people are motivated without coercion. The Spanish philosopher and statesman Ortega Y Gasset called this unique political quality "opinion."[21] Public opinion is central for political life. That is why even dictators worry more about what people believe, think, and claim than what they know. All authoritarian governments depend on spying on their citizens and waging campaigns of misinformation and disinformation.

At the heart of politics, then, is power. What is power? In simple terms, it is the ability to make things happen with access to the means of doing so.

The simplest means for human beings is our body and its reach. The human transition into cultural life—with its resources of language, writing, and technology—led to the ability of human beings to reach each other, other creatures, and things beyond the location of our physical bodies. The human world, in other words, is not only infused with power but also the expression of it. Where power is positive, it enables others to make things happen that affect their lives and others in the form of flourishing. The now banal term for this is "empowerment." Where power is negative, it is horded and results in the disempowering of others. Colonialism, enslavement, racism, sexism, and varieties of other forms of dehumanization and exploitation are forms of disempowering of others through the concentration of powers in special groups. Here, we see a source of great tension—namely, the relationship of rule to politics. Oppressive regimes seek rule over politics.

This dichotomy of rule and politics makes concrete the well-known distinction between what is known over the past few hundred years as the right and the left. The rightwing tends to aim for rule over politics and the leftwing tends to focus on politics more than rule. Oddly enough, this tends to lead to a more concrete distinction in which the right, even when they disavow government, tend to concentrate on law and order, especially in the forms of force, and the left tend to focus on protest and other activities of speech. This connects even more to their responses to moments of social crisis. The impulse of the right is to reestablish order, which always takes the form of a "return" to a supposedly perfect past. The left are divided on this issue. The basic premise of the left is that getting better takes the form of proliferating freedom. Thus, to return to a perfect order would be antithetical to such goals. Looking to the past, the left see people struggling to create a better future. The past, in other words, was never perfect. Moreover, looking at the past and moments of crisis, the left's aim of proliferating freedom leads inevitably to the distinction between liberty and freedom. Liberty involves the absence of obstacles. The kind of left that focuses on liberty, therefore, often regards government (rule) and at times even society and politics (social world, speech, and power) as threats to liberty. Freedom, however, is complicated. It involves cultivating the ability to make things happen, which means it requires power as empowerment and processes of growth. It also does not regard society as an enemy but instead a necessary condition for human flourishing, which is treated as a rich sense of freedom and other normative aims such as health, justice, and other aims beyond that such as, as we have seen, *MAat*, in addition to others such as *Ubuntu, Uhuru, he* (和), etc.[22]

Liberation *from* and Liberation *for*

We return, then, to the question of liberation. As with our discussion of decolonization and decoloniality, liberation raises not only the question of its negative movement—liberation *from*—but also, in agreement with Catherine

Walsh, its positive one—liberation *for*. The libertarian left tend to be suspicious of the second formulation, which for them often means the personalizing of what to do once liberation *from* is achieved. This position tends to work well with liberalism, and as that, in its neoliberal, neoconservative, and even conservative forms, stands to the right of liberation *for*; it is no accident that the libertarian left have a history, in countries such as Australia, Canada, the United Kingdom, and the United States, of allying with the right. This relativism of right and left also means that other forms of left could articulate positions that result in the interests of the right. The critical discussion of moralism, for instance, raises this problem. Moralized subjects in societies where one could only have a legitimate public voice only as a victim undermine the category of political subjects, whose "voice" is a function of political conditions of appearance. What is the difference? Victimization belongs properly to moral and legal resolutions, but political agency belongs to participation in the production of power for all—in a word, citizenship. Liberation *from* is a response to harm; liberation *for* is the rallying of creative resources of possibility.

Under Euromodern rule, the harms of colonialism, enslavement, and racism required impositions of rule, which barred politics in the lives upon those whom they were imposed. This was one of Steve Bantu Biko's insights on the South African apartheid state. To maintain itself, it waged a war not only against non-white peoples but also against politics because to maintain itself, it had to prioritize rule at the expense of political life. Blocking politics required barring political life from certain groups of people. This involved making them invisible. This invisibility took at least four forms.[23]

One is racial, which focuses on quantity. There are always "too many" members of a racially degraded group around, which makes them what the French call *de trop* (roughly, unnecessary, unwanted, or unsuitable). The significance of this for critical discourses of diversity should be evident. It is one of the reasons why diversity could be celebrated in some institutions in which only one member of a despised group has limited access.

Another is temporal. Where settler colonialism claims victory, Indigenous people "belong" to the past. This makes their continued presence a ghostly one. The settler's longing for a future devoid of the Indigenous peoples occasions anxiety over their continued presence.

A third goes directly to the heart of politics: speech. Such people are ignored when they speak. Not heard, they, in effect, have no voice. This is historically a heavily gendered experience in European and many Asian countries in which to speak was a properly male phenomenon. (Oddly enough, I typed the previous sentence right before a session at a conference in which a group of male participants simply started speaking to each other while a female participant was responding to one of the gentlemen's papers!) Elaborating the details of the history of voice and why it was different in many pre-Euromodern colonial societies of the Global South would take us far afield. The main thing is that this invisibility is predominantly female in Euromodern societies and those affected by them, which are the foci of this chapter.

A fourth is epistemological. It is the presumed illegitimacy of non-Euromodern knowledge. Elsewhere, I refer to this phenomenon as *epistemic closure*.[24] It is a form of presumed knowing in which there is, where a particular group is identified, nothing more to know or learn.

The imposition of these forms of oppressive invisibility entails liberation *from* them. Liberation *for* a society without those dynamics entails a world of no people who are always *de trop* by virtue of their race, barred from the future by virtue of being indigenous, voiceless because blocked from embodying political agency or citizenship by virtue of their gender or race, and excluded from the production and appearance of and contributing to knowledge. There are, of course, other forms of invisibility, but I have chosen these four because of their familiarity in both colonial countries and postcolonies of Euromodernity. The fourth, which focuses on knowledge, also raises radical questions of the conditions of thought and norms of thinking and living. Radicalized, it raises the question of justifications. After all, the decolonial challenge is whether even modes of knowing and even being normatively moved in such societies are also disempowering.[25] It demands, then, questioning even liberation, which is why the Wits University Centre for Diversity Studies' formulation of "liberation*s*" was also a demand for radical self-critique.

A Consideration by Way of Concluding

At this point, I would like to close with a consideration in light of the tensions I have outlined. The distinction between rule and politics raises correlative expectations of human relationships premised on presuppositions of what people are and how we are affected and how we think. I use the word "affected" here because, as I hope needs no elaboration, rationality and reason are not the sole bases of human action. This does not mean that irrationality is the remaining recourse. The presupposition of rule is the construction of order through repetition that, in turn, is premised on similarity. This is a basic element of form and order, since that involves consistency of a principle or element of a system. In effect, then, inconsistency is that which contradicts the system and, thus, belongs "outside." As a condition of social belonging, it means, in effect, that like belongs with like. Radicalized, it achieves maximum consistency through the elimination of difference. Such a system has no room for genuine others, since sufficient likeness requires another instance of the same. As a condition of love, from such a perspective, there is simply the advancement of an analog. To love is to demand the other becoming an affirmation of oneself. Brought to the level of society, we are back in the terrain of moralism, where a search for moral purity ultimately collapses into a celebration of the self as the standard of all. It begins with a model of "us" versus "them," but it eventually arrives at "you" versus "me," and then there is, finally, "I" versus "me," and then eventually just "I...," but even the ellipsis signifies something that is not-I, which must be eliminated. Brought entirely out of relations, there is no one and nothing from which or through which to distinguish the self and, thus, facilitate appearance. Put differently, there is eventually nothing.

Such a negative outcome requires reaching back through the reiteration of the penultimate sequence, but by then there is just repetition of the self. Although this is an abstract exercise, it is a summary of models of love premised on similarity and the presumption of intelligibility only through similitude and, eventually, sameness. It is the core of the expression: "I belong with, and could only love, my own kind." This mentality extends, as is well known, even to images of the divine.

In her extraordinary essay, "The God of Love and Affliction," the French philosopher Simone Weil reflects that affliction is a social form of suffering in which enslavement brings to the fore its significance. She writes: "The ancients, who knew this question very well, would say, 'A man loses half his soul the day he becomes a slave.'"[26] The question remains, what would she or he do with the other half? Some fight, others retreat and lose more. Others love. None of these are simple. Weil offers this observation on love:

> Lovers and friends have two desires. One is to love so much that one enters the other to make a single being. The other is to love so much that with half the earthly globe between them, their union would not suffer any diminishment.... Those impossible desires are within us as a mark of our destination, and it is good for us when we don't hope to accomplish them.[27]

Weil's first formulation graphically brings forth the implications of assimilation. It is a core element not only of one dominant model of love but also ethics and morality. It extends also beyond those categories into the normative implications of theodicy, as I outlined it above in the example of perversity's systemic completeness and the production of those who must have everything, which by extension includes everyone. Weil's second observation is intriguing, as it is premised on distance and separation that paradoxically produce "impossible desire." Impossibility here is rhetorical, since, as the example shows so well, what is supposedly impossible happens, and it happens with sufficient regularity to be familiar. There are people who love a deity, for instance, that not only could never be in their image but also with the conviction that such a deity should never be such.

How are such acts possible? Additionally, what is the relationship between them and politics? Do they have something also to do with liberations?

We have already done much of the groundwork for the political significance of these questions. Rule as an exemplification of the first desire raises the question of politics as that of the second. Politics involves contingency and flourishing the result of which is a limitation of knowledge before performance and outcomes. Politics, in other words, requires the possibility of difference coming into being. Radicalized, difference is unintelligible.

A concrete example of this is slavery in the United States. Imagine an enslaved African woman there in the late 18th or early 19th century. Given the practice of institutional slavery across much of the globe, she faced a world that imposed a single thesis: nothing she said, thought, or felt mattered. As enslaved, she supposedly had no value beyond her extracted labor, the pleasures that could be sought from her flesh, and the profit for which she was sold as a commodity. Yet she—and as many of such people remain anonymous except where "found" through archaeological or historical research—*acted*, and her actions reverberated into directions she could not have possibly predicted. The descendants of her actions could not have emerged without her actions. As many versions of her remain anonymous, we should bear in mind that so, too, to her were the descendants of those actions. We today were anonymous to those of the past from the simple fact of our not having yet been born, and we should also bear in mind that those who dominated the past presumed, with certainty, their analogical reproduction in the form of the first desire Weil posed.

Here, I think an illustration from the life of Frederick Douglass, the famed abolitionist, statesman, and political thinker, may be illuminating. Born an enslaved child under the name Frederick Augustus Washington Bailey in 1818, "Douglass" was the name he chose during his period of fugitivity when he escaped from Maryland to New York. He struggled to articulate his life experience on many occasions, but three were brought to print in book form. The first was *Narrative of the Life of Frederick Douglass, an American Slave* (1845). The second was *My Bondage and My Freedom* (1855). And the final was *The Life and Times of Frederick Douglass* (1881). Douglass was a fugitive at the publication of the first. His crime? He "stole" his master's "property"—himself.

The contradiction of being property capable of stealing itself is a paradox, to say the least. As U.S. copyright law dated back to 1790, Douglass's first book added to this conundrum since it was protected under U.S. law even though its author was not. His book had rights that he lacked. The book's details endangered him of extradition to Maryland, to re-enslavement by the Auld family, his "owners."

Douglass found refuge in England and Ireland, where his supporters brokered a deal with Hugh Auld for his manumission in 1846. Legally "free," Douglass returned to the United States, where he devoted his life first to the continued struggle against legalized slavery, which led to his involvement in the U.S. Civil War and then to the fight against its structural reassertion in the United States and abroad, including in the Caribbean during his years as ambassador to Haiti (1889–1891). Fighting against slavery meant for Douglass a fight *for* freedom. For Douglass, this included women's struggles, in which he was involved as early as the women's rights Seneca Falls convention of 1848. His commitment never wavered. Accompanying these struggles was also a reflection that he elaborated and moved to a location of centrality in his later autobiographical writings. It is the story of Harriet Bailey, his mother.

Douglass was separated from his mother at birth and placed, along with other enslaved children, under the care of Betsy Bailey, his enslaved elderly grandmother. In the *Narrative*, he claimed he saw his mother Harriet only a few times and developed no emotional attachment to her. Its rhetorical purpose was perhaps to emphasize the cruelty of slavery. That motif of a lack of emotional attachment has unfortunately persisted even into contemporary narratives of paternal abandonment in black families. The rationale is that of continued trauma across generations from past fathers being sold off. I often have to remind those who endorse that explanation that they fail to account for the fact that mothers were sold away, too—hence the emergence of a spiritual such as "Sometimes I Feel Like a Motherless Child" (from the 1870s)—and that many fathers, as was Douglass's, turned out to be their white masters.

In *The Life and Times of Frederick Douglass*, he tells a different story under the chapter title "Troubles of Childhood." Taken from his grandmother to labor at the house of Lt. Lloyd around the age of seven, he was introduced to the full brutality of enslavement. As things turned out, his mother Harriet worked on the fields of a plantation twelve miles away. Learning of her child's location, she walked the distance in the evenings to spend time with him into dawn, when she returned to the fields. On the last occasion, she came to his rescue from the cruel, enslaved cook who abused him. She soon thereafter passed away.

Children, as any child psychologist would attest, cannot understand parental absence. Even where the parent is enslaved, the child's point of view is to blame the parent, just as poverty, war, and other sources of separation do not always lead to forgiveness from offspring who experience absence as abandonment. That Douglass's mother endured hardship to see him—walking those nights through rural Maryland was a perilous venture—compelled this reflection in his later years:

> My mother had walked twelve miles to see me and had the same distance to travel over again before the sunrise. I do not remember ever seeing her again. Her death soon ended the little communication that had existed between us, and with it, I believe, a life full of weariness and heartfelt sorrow. To me, it has ever been a grief that I knew my mother so little and have so few of her words treasured in my remembrance. I have since learned that she was the only one of all the colored people of Tuckahoe who could read. How she acquired this knowledge I know not, for Tuckahoe was the last place in the world where she would have been likely to find facilities for learning. I can, therefore, fondly and proudly ascribe to her, an earnest love of knowledge. That a field-hand should learn to read in any slave State is remarkable, but the achievement of my

mother, considering the place and circumstances, was very extraordinary. In view of this fact, I am happy to attribute any love of letters I may have, not to my presumed Anglo-Saxon paternity, but to the native genius of my sable, unprotected, and uncultivated mother—a woman who belonged to a race whose mental endowments are still disparaged and despised.[28]

The world in which the child Frederick lived was one in which he was valued only as property. To be valued was to be of use to the master or to whomever the master leased him. He was a commodity, a thing of market value. His point of view did not matter. His wants, his desires, his dreams, nothing *from him* was of value except whatever those who used him wanted from him. For enslaved women and men, this included their flesh since, as many chronicles attest, they were also sources of sexual gratification and other forms of physical amusement. Yet Harriet Bailey managed, in her efforts, to introduce her child to something up to that point he had not imagined: love.

Douglass's value as far as he knew, even as a child, was as a commodity. Love, however, offered a different kind of value; it is a judgment on existence against being. It is, in effect, to say that being is of immeasurably less value without the beloved. In her extraordinary efforts to spend time with her child, Harriet showed she loved him. In doing so, she was also saying, "Frederick, you're valuable."

Love offered Frederick a glimpse of a possibility beyond black resignation and enslavement since it is a relationship to which one *belongs*.

Yet if that were all that Frederick learned from Harriet's efforts, there would be a loss. Knowing he was valuable could have made him a cocky slave who believed himself better than others among the enslaved. It could have made him, when manumitted, an obnoxious freedman who regarded himself as an exception among other blacks. He could have had pride. But would he have had dignity?

The enslaved child's world was clear. Only masters bestow value. What, then, is the value of being loved by an enslaved woman? If he was an exception, what was she? If the enslaved child rejected her love, he would have retroactively forfeited the value of any love he offered, since the basis would be the same: love from a slave is not valuable. It was not sufficient, then, to be loved by Harriet. Frederick had to value that love. That spark of love and the flame that grew from valuing it nurtured a revolutionary spirit. Frederick went on to learn to read and write, fight against the slave breaker Reverend Covey, eventually escape from Maryland, and, despite the liberties afforded him in the shadows under his new name of Frederick Douglass, throw himself into the struggle for abolition and the subsequent political lifelong fight for the living practice of freedom. His love of freedom was also an expression of his love for his mother.

Douglass's story is a path from an enslaved being to a black to what Steve Bantu Biko and many other Black revolutionaries called Black consciousness.

Its message is clear. The movement to Black consciousness requires valuing being valued by the damned of the earth.

We would be remiss, however, if we were to end this reflection with Douglass's consciousness and political work. It is Harriet Bailey's story to consider here, for the question remains: why did she act? She knew of the child but had not known him. What brought her to devote those six months to a child for whom it was possible that her act of devotion would never be appreciated? Given her death shortly thereafter, she had no way of knowing that he would become *Frederick Douglass*. There was no epistemic messenger. There was no sign of the system of slavery being overturned. Yet, she *acted*.

Concluding Considerations

A crucial feature of political commitment is that it is an existential paradox. Unlike moral commitment, which involves doing the "right thing," political commitment affords no advanced notice or assured principle of verification. Her actions could have produced an arrogant child who is shortly thereafter killed, or a fighting, committed spirit who suffers the same fate. Political commitment requires acting without knowing the outcome and acting for those whom one ultimately will never know. A six-months' glimpse into the life of the child is not the same as knowing the man he was to become. This insight is similar with regard to political action. No political act offers guarantees save one: it will affect others whom one would ultimately never know. What, then, could one hope for with such action?

The first thing to consider hits the heart of critical diversity. Those who benefit from our actions may be so radically different from us that we may even recoil at the discovery of whom they turn out to be.

Second, those who suffer from our actions may be those beyond our expectations.

Third, the first and second considerations lead to the realization that the epistemic act of trying to imagine the recipients of our actions collapses into the first desire of love, which would be an affirmation of the self. Put differently, it would involve simply positing versions of ourselves into a future whose condition of possibility requires the emergence of people who are both not us and also, possibly, not like us.

Fourth, this means acknowledging, through political commitment, the production of freedom that transcends us. This act of political commitment is simultaneously a manifestation of the second form of love. It offers the paradox of loving, by virtue of action, anonymous generations to come.[29]

The fourth kind raises the question of building a future, even in the face of circumstances that do not guarantee our having one. In effect, the message, politically understood, is this: learn we hope, but try we must.

Notes

1. *(Re)Imagining Liberations: Institutionalised Despair*Critical Hope*, The Wits Centre for Diversity Studies (WiCDS), Johannesburg, South Africa, August 6–8, 2018.
2. For elaboration, see Lewis R. Gordon, "Afro-Jewish Ethics?" in Curtis Hutt, Berel Dov Lerrner, and Julia Schwartzmann (eds.), *Jewish Religious and Philosophical Ethics* (London, UK: Routledge, 2018), 213–227 and "Juifs contre la Libération: Une critique afro-juive," *Tumultes* numéro 50 (2018): 97–108.
3. For an elaboration of this problem, see the succeeding chapter as well as Ato Sekyi-Otu, *Left Universalism, Africacentric Essays* (New York, NY: Routledge, 2018), and Drucilla Cornell, *Law and Revolution in South Africa: uBuntu, Dignity, and the Struggle for Constitutional Transformation* (New York, NY: Fordham University Press, 2014).
4. See, e.g., W.E.B. Du Bois, *Black Reconstruction in America, 1860–1880* (New York, NY: Harcourt, Brace and Company, 1938 [1935]); David Roediger, *The Wages of Wages of Whiteness: Race and the Making of the American Working Class*, New Edition (London, UK: Verso, 1999); and Jane Anna Gordon, *Statelessness and Contemporary Enslavement* (New York, NY: Routledge, 2020).
5. For discussion of this problem, see Lewis R. Gordon, *Existentia Africana: Understanding Africana Existential Thought* (New York, NY: Routledge, 2000), Chapter 2, and *Introduction to Africana Philosophy* (Cambridge, UK: Cambridge University Press, 2008), introduction.
6. A list of the many influential writings in this area of thought would be too long. Although there is a rich history of theorizing decolonization in African and African diasporic thought—see, for example, Ngũgĩ wa Thiong'o's *Decolonising the Mind: the Politics of Language in African Literature* (Nairobi, Kenya: Heinemann Kenya, 1986), and my *An Introduction to Africana Philosophy*—it is the Latin American line that has become hegemonic in the academy. For a genealogy and recent critical discussion, see Walter Mignolo and Catherine Walsh, *On Decoloniality: Concepts, Analytics, Praxis* (Durham, NC: Duke University Press, 2018). See also Julia Suàrez-Krabbe, *Race, Rights and Rebels: Alternatives beyond Human Rights and Development* (London, UK: Rowman & Littlefield International, 2015), and Ricardo Sanín-Restrepo, *Decolonizing Democracy* (London, UK; Rowman & Littlefield International, 2016).
7. Frantz Fanon, *Les Damnés de la terre* (Paris, France: François Maspero, 1961), Chapter 1. I refer to this text throughout as *The Damned of the Earth*. For elaboration and discussion, see Lewis R. Gordon, *What Fanon Said: A Philosophical Introduction to His Life and Thought* (New York, NY: Fordham UP; London, UK: Hurst; Johannesburg, South Africa: Wits University Press, 2015).
8. For elaboration through conversations with a global group of decolonial theorists, see Sayan Dey (ed.), *Different Spaces, Different Voices: A Rendezvous with Decoloniality* (Mumbai, India: Becomeshakespear.com, 2018).
9. I explore such phenomena in Part I and Part III of *Bad Faith and Antiblack Racism*, 2nd Edition (London, UK: Humanity Books, 2021). See also Jean-Paul Sartre's *Being and Nothingness*, trans. Hazel Barnes (New York, NY: Washington Square Press, 1956), Part III, and Barnaby B. Barratt, *Sexual Health and Erotic Freedom* (Bloomington, IN: Xlibris, 2005).
10. I state "for the most part" since, of course, there are exceptions such as Rozena Maart's "Exordium: Writing and the Relation: From Textual Coloniality to South African Black Consciousness," in Monica Michlin and Jean-Paul Rocchi (eds.), *Black Intersectionalities: A Critique for the 21st Century* (Liverpool, UK: Liverpool University Press, 2013), 21–33.
11. See Catherine Walsh's chapter "The Decolonial *For*: Resurgences, Shifts, and Movements," in Walter Mignolo and Catherine Walsh, *On Decoloniality*, 15–32.

12. For elaboration of this conception of universal as equal access, see Ato Sekyi-Otu, *Left Universalism, Africacentric Essays*.
13. This is not an exclusively left-oriented critique. For a similar observation from a conservative perspective, see Jack Kerwick, *Misguided Guardians: The Conservative Case Against Neoconservatism* (Las Vegas, NV: Stairway Press, 2016).
14. Karl Jaspers, *The Question of German Guilt*, trans. E.B. Ashton (New York, NY: Fordham University Press, 2000); Steve Bantu Biko, *I Write What I Like: Selected Writings* (Chicago, IL: University of Chicago Press, 2002); Iris Marion Young, "Responsibility and Global Labor Justice," *The Journal of Political Philosophy* 12, no. 4 (2004): 365–388 and *Responsibility for Justice* (New York, NY: Oxford University Press, 2011); and Lewis R. Gordon, "Iris Marion Young on Political Responsibility: A Reading through Jaspers and Fanon," *Symposia on Gender, Race, and Philosophy* 3, no. 1 (January 2007): http://web.mit.edu/sgrp and *Fear of Black Consciousness* (New York, NY: Farrar, Straus and Giroux; London, UK: Penguin Press, 2021).
15. For more on this concept, see Lewis R. Gordon, "Shifting the Geography of Reason in an Age of Disciplinary Decadence," *Transmodernity: Journal of Peripheral Cultural Production of the Luso-Hispanic World* 1, no. 2 (2011): 96–104.
16. Again, see K. Anthony Appiah's critical discussion of the "West" as a European construction: "There Is No Such Thing as Western Civilization," *The Guardian* (9 November 2016): https://www.theguardian.com/world/2016/nov/09/western-civilisation-appiah-reith-lecture?CMP=share_btn_fb
17. In Chapter 1, I mentioned some ancient African female writers. In addition to *Writings from Ancient Egypt*, trans. Toby Wilkinson (London, UK: Penguin Classics, 2016), which includes writings from the Old Kingdom (c. 2686–2181 BCE) but primarily those from the Middle Kingdom (c. 1975 BC–1640 BCE) and New Kingdom (c. 1570–c.1069 BCE), see also, for more recent ancient women's writings, Roger S. Bagnall and Raffaela Cribiore (eds.), *Women's Letters from Ancient Egypt, 300 BC–AD 800* (Ann Arbor, MI: University of Michigan Press, 2015).
18. "Inscription of Antef," 12th Dynasty, Kmt/Ancient Egypt, 1991–1782 BCE. See discussion in Chapter 1. Also see Théophile Obeng in his "Egypt: Ancient History of African Philosophy," in Wiredu (ed.), *A Companion to African Philosophy* (Malden, MA: Blackwell, 2004), 35, and Heinrich Brugsch (ed.), *Thesaurus Inscriptionum Aegyptiacarum: Woerterbuch Suppl.*, 6 vols. (Leipsig, Germany: Graz, 1883–1891).
19. See, e.g., Lorraine Boissoneault, "Colored Pigments and Complex Tools Suggest Humans Were Trading 100,000 Years Earlier Than Previously Believed," *Smithsonian Magazine* (March 15, 2018): https://www.smithsonianmag.com/science-nature/colored-pigments-and-complex-tools-suggest-human-trade-100000-years-earlier-previously-believed-180968499/; Matt Ridley, *The Rational Optimist: How Prosperity Evolves*, Reprint Edition (London, UK: Harper Perennial, 2011); Yval Noah Harari, *Sapiens: A Brief History of Humankind* (London, UK: Harper Perennial, 2018). And, of course, the classic overview of the history of theoretical economics, Robert L. Heilbroner's classic, *The Worldly Philosophers: The Lives, Times, and Ideas of the Great Economic*, Revised 7th Edition (New York, NY: Simon & Schuster, 1999 [original 1953]).
20. This logic of whites ultimately defending themselves from victimization through enslaving others goes back to John Locke's defense of slavery in his *Second Treatise on Government* (1689). It continues in contemporary white racist rationalizations; for discussion, see, e.g., Joe Feagin, *The White Racial Frame: Centuries of Racial Framing and Counter-Framing*, 2nd Edition (New York, NY: Routledge, 2013).
21. José Ortega y Gasset, *The Revolt of the Masses* (New York, NY: W.W. Norton, 1994 [1930]).

22. For elaboration of these concepts, see Mabogo More, *Looking through Philosophy in Black: Memoirs* (London, UK: Rowman & Littlefield International, 2018); Ato Sekyi-Otu, *Left Universalism, Africacentric Essays*; Drucilla Cornell, *Law and Revolution in South Africa*; Magobe B. Ramose, *African Philosophy through Ubuntu* (Harare, ZI: Mond Books, 1999); Kwasi Wiredu (ed.), *A Companion to African Philosophy*; and for connections with other normative concepts across the Global South, see Fernanda Frizzo Bragato and Lewis R. Gordon (eds.), *Geopolitics and Decolonization: Perspectives from the Global South* (London, UK: Rowman & Littlefield International, 2018); Mignolo and Walsh, *On Decoloniality*; Julia Suàrez-Krabbe, *Race, Rights and Rebels*; and Ricardo Sanín-Restrepo, *Decolonizing Democracy*.

23. I offer brief summaries here; for their elaboration, see *Fear of Black Consciousness*.

24. I introduced this concept in 1995 in *Fanon and the Crisis of European Man: An Essay in Philosophy and the Human Sciences* (New York, NY: Routledge). See the 2nd Edition, also published by Routledge, which offers a set of critical essays addressing epistemic closure and other themes such as anonymity, the extraordinary achievement of everyday life, tragic revolutionary violence, disciplinary decadence, and more.

25. In addition to Walsh and Mignolo's *On Decoloniality*, see Boaventura de Sousa Santos, *Epistemologies of the South: Justice against Epistemicide* (New York, NY: Routledge, 2014) and *The End of the Cognitive Empire: The Coming of Age of Epistemologies of the South* (Durham, NC: Duke University Press, 2018) for recent studies of this problem.

26. Simone Weil, "The God of Love and Affliction," in George A. Panichas (ed.), *The Simone Weil Reader* (New York, NY: Kingston, RI: Moyer Bell, 1985), 439.

27. Weil, "The God of Love and Affliction," 446.

28. Frederick Douglass, *The Life and Times of Frederick Douglass* (Radford, VA: Wilder Publications, 2008 [1881]), 16.

29. For more on political dimensions of anticolonial love, see Asma Abbas, *Another Love: A Politics of the Unrequited* (Lanham, MD: Lexington Books, 2018).

Chapter 3

Toward the Decolonization of Normative Life

> Reforms and revolutions are created by the illogical actions of people. Very few logical people ever make reforms and none make revolutions. Rights are what you make and what you take.
>
> —James Boggs, *Pages from a Black Radical's Notebook*[1]

There is a problem that surfaces in many struggles for social transformation in the name of justice. The standard position is this: struggles for liberation are fought against injustice. Societies in which such struggles are waged are, in other words, unjust. Fixing them requires eliminating injustice. This injustice is often about those who have versus those who lack. Those who have are often "the few," though in some cases, they are also a fairly large majority, as is the case of the designated white populations of Europe and North America. Sometimes those who do not have are minorities, as is the case of immigrants, mostly of color, in much of the so-called developed world. In the so-called underdeveloped countries, those who lack are the overwhelming majority. And in the first quarter of the 21st century, those who have less are the planet's majority. Advantages, in other words, are clearly on the side of a group of global elites. Justice is not, then, exclusively about numbers. The question, from this point of view, is to make right what was wrong. The effort is to make things just.

What happens, however, if a struggle is fought, an evil institution has lost, and yet what remains is social misery? Is it correct to say justice was not achieved?

Many important, historical struggles have been waged in the name of justice. There were the Civil War and the Civil Rights Struggle in the United States. There was the outlawing of slavery on the high seas of the British Empire. There were the French Revolution and the Haitian Revolution that attempted to make the French supposedly true to their ideals. There were the many independence and transformation struggles across Africa, Asia, and Abya Yala in the last half of the 20th century with the anti-Apartheid struggle in South Africa standing as one of the shining, though currently troubled, examples.[2] There were too many to mention here, and there are others continuing across the globe such as those for blacks and First nation peoples not only in the northern countries but also those of the Global South.

A problem with many struggles is that victory is often misunderstood as the moment of replacing one group of leaders with another. Frantz Fanon, the famed revolutionary psychiatrist and philosopher, called this "the process of decolonization." On replacing one group with another, it was not the achievement of freedom, though it exemplified a form of liberation. It was only the beginning of the true struggle. Fanon also cautioned against trapping normative thought in what he called "Greco-Latin" or Greek and Roman pedestals. By this, he meant closing our minds off from other than now hegemonic Western ways of understanding the normative world.[3] We fight for justice, but what if justice is not enough?

This depends on the problem at hand. To understand the problem being addressed here, we need to look at the concept of what, as we have seen, Aníbal Quijano and others call "coloniality."[4] This concept addresses colonialism as a form of power aimed at the domination of all reality. This is something many African diasporic thinkers noticed as far back as the 18th century.[5] We could also see elements of it from Christopher Columbus's journals and the 15th through early 16th century Spanish priest Bartolomé Las Casas's critical reflections on the avowed conquest of Abya Yala.[6] As that which aims at the conquest of all reality, colonialism becomes a system whose goal is not only conquest but also the offering of the domination of life and the assertion of itself as ontological and the primacy of ontology.[7] Thus, knowledge is, as nearly all decolonial theorists have argued, implicated here in the form of epistemic colonization.[8] Fanon observed in *Black Skin, White Masks* that this quest was radical in scope because it enchained what people think and *how* they think. We could say the same thing about norms and normative thought—namely, our understanding of what it means to be good, to do things right, to make the world such that it is, upon reflection, the best we could and *ought* to achieve.

The logic of norms is not an easy case to address, as is that of knowledge. Many decolonial critics, except perhaps María Lugones, Nelson Maldonado-Torres, Boaventura de Sousa Santos, Julia Suárez-Krabbe, Ricardo Sanín-Restrepo, and Catherine Walsh, for example, see the metacritical question of norms in almost exclusively epistemological terms.[9] This means that *what* and *how* for these critics become matters of what we *think*. So, to free our thought means also to free our norms. Maldonado-Torres, drawing on Fanon and others in the Black radical tradition, argues for establishing genuinely ethical relationships beyond the ontological (being) and epistemological (knowledge); de Sousa Santos, through is work on pluralistic epistemologies of the social world, law, and theology, argues for counter-hegemonic models of human rights; Lugones, Sanín-Restrepo, Suárez-Krabbe, and Walsh, exploring the same and Indigenous Abya Yala sources, appeal to a revealed nakedness through which colonial norms—which Lugones and Walsh, building on Quijano, call *coloniality*, Sanín-Restrepo calls the *encryption of power*, and Suárez-Krabbe calls *the death project*—are revealed in a call beyond Eurocentrism and androcentrism in conceptions of legitimacy and authority of a radical, activist-oriented scope that links human beings with a broad spectrum of reality.

Some thoughts immediately come to mind. The first is that appeals to establishing genuinely ethical relationships often take the form of "fixing" people, making them into better human beings, in a way that often reeks of moralism. This phenomenon often leads to the search for human purity, with the inevitable effect of purging the world of infelicitous and unsavory people. Something seems awry or at least lost sight of here. Is the problem that there are bad people in the world? Or is there another consideration—namely, that there are a sufficient number of bad people with the power to enforce their wills over many if not most others? If such power relations were changed, would it still matter that there are bad people in the world?

I once argued with an environmental activist who insisted that we could make the world better if we—everyone—acted on her or his moral conscience. In response, I asked her what would bother her more—to be considered immoral or stupid? Without hesitation, she regarded being considered stupid to be worse. If that is so, what hope do we have for those in the financial or business sectors or those seeking professional advancement and recognition when they face situations in which to act morally would be considered stupid by their peers? And even if we concede her point that a world in which *everyone* did the right thing might be good, we would face the reality that such a world would not have the problems at hand in the first place. For the problem to rise, there has to be some people who do *not* act from their conscience, which makes the question of why they do not, especially where doing such is marked by perceived intelligence conjoined with moral worth, the central one to consider. That question requires addressing the incentives, which points back to a society that may actually reward unconscionable behavior.[10]

Such concerns lead to radical questions such as our responsibility for morality and, even more, ethical life, especially where being esteemed as smart instead of moral is more important. It is where the distinction between ethics and morality come to the fore. In the former, our responsibility is for ethics itself—we are responsible, in other words, for responsibility.

An additional question is this: how radical should the transformation of norms be? What if even ethical relationships are, at ground level, colonized *by colonial normative life*? Are we willing to take on the decolonization of normative life?

Fanon raised this problem in a different way. He noticed how many critics and activists formulated struggles against racism. They saw it in terms of recognition and the formation of ethical relationships between the Self and the Other. Racism, he argued is the project of trying to make other groups of people into things that are not the self (indeed, not even capable of being a self) and not the Other (because an Other is also a self).[11] Such an effort poses problems for ethics and morals. Ethical relationships depend on the Self–Other dialectic. An obligation by definition is toward someone, even if that turns out to be oneself. Even such things as property and material things depend ultimately on a world of social relations through which to answer to one's treatment of such objects.[12] And in terms of morals—that is, the set of rules and regulations serving as standards of conduct—they, too, require the relation of selves and others. Even the rule-obsessed Immanuel Kant, who ultimately argued for understanding obligation through respect for moral laws themselves, ultimately appealed to a Kingdom of Ends in which there are rational beings all equal by virtue of no one being able to stand as an exception to Moral Law or Absolute Obligation—in other words, *the* Categorical Imperative.[13] What, however, could people situated or *forced* outside of that dialectic do with regard to ethics and moral obligation?

Reflection radicalizes the problem. If they attempt to establish an ethical relationship, they must do so by the rules (morals) of a society premised on their exclusion. Thus, if they attempt to enter the ethical sphere of that society, the already included people treat the excluded ones as *violating the ethical space by virtue of doing the same to the avowedly moral rules.* Fanon's name for this was controversial. He called it "violence."

Colonized and racially subordinated people commit "violence" simply by appearing. If to appear is to be a participant in the moral space—a space whose legitimacy is built on such people's exclusion—then the problem becomes a violation of what was presumed "just." In other words, the system presumed their exclusion was just. Thus, their inclusion in that system would be a form of injustice. History offers many examples of this dynamic. When Fanon said decolonization is always violent, he was pointing to the presumptive justice of colonial and settler societies. The only just condition they would accept is the maintenance of the status quo or, worse, the annihilation of the Indigenous peoples. Thus, transformation, decolonization, is for such governors intrinsically unjust. A similar logic applies to a social remedy such as affirmative action. If the dominant group's advantages are just and systematically linked to the disadvantages of other groups in that society, then the dominant group's disadvantages are just. To transform that would therefore be unjust. Yes, something is awry here.

The immediate response is to see this as a relativizing of justice. It is about the justice of the dominators versus the justice of the dominated. In black thought, this could be read as a series of double conscious moments. The first is to see, as we have seen, a system that regards its practices of exclusion as just. Thus, blacks are excluded because blacks are presumed infelicitous or, simply, bad. Blacks are excluded because it is supposedly right to exclude them. Blacks are, in other words, "problems." If blacks discover the problem of being made into problems, if blacks learn that there is a society that places everything in favor of whites—white wealth, for example, was produced by a societal commitment to, in the form of governing institutions being harnessed for the purpose of, white supremacy—then they could conclude that blacks are not the problem; the society is the problem (unjust) and it must be changed.[14] As I have been arguing throughout, this reflective, dialectical stage is potentiated double consciousness.[15]

Legal theorist Kimberlé Crenshaw adds to this argument an important insight in her intersectional theory of harm. Imagine an automobile collision at a four-way intersection in a world in which harm only occurs to the property. Authorities arriving on the scene would simply examine the damaged vehicles to determine what harm has occurred. Now imagine that in that world, only owners of the property can be harmed, and only white males can own property. It follows that only white males can suffer harm. The investigators need simply to look at the damaged cars and then into them or research their ownership to determine whether a white male was injured (even if there were white women, women of color, and men of color in any of the vehicles). Add white females to those who are violable, and a similar logic follows. Oddly enough, in the historic world of Euromodern colonialism, often the animal pets of white men and women counted among those who could be harmed, and we are already familiar with Euromodern common law and legal code systems that counted corporations as persons over and against people of color.[16] In a world where people of color are included in the category of those who could suffer harm, the intersectional interpretation of the four-way collision offers more possibilities for the examination of harm. Notice in this analysis that Crenshaw does not discount white males who are harmed. The main point is that it *includes* a broader range of others.[17]

An error of the old system is the presumed universality of whites and the normative world that supports white supremacy. Particularizing whites reveals a larger world of human possibility—one that includes nonwhite peoples. This larger world reaches for universality in its practices, but it understands that it is a relational world since in principle it need not stop at nonwhites. Many (if not most) whites had before presumed they *are the world*. Thus, they supposedly needed not be in a relationship with anyone beyond other whites. They remained, at the logic of norms, among themselves. Other groups saw themselves, on the other hand, *in relation to whites and each other*. They, thus, knew they were not "the world." Learning that whites are also not actually the world means to understand a bigger reality in which knowledge reveals more but never its entirety. This humility calls for a *universalizing* practice that is never *the universal*.

We now simply have to consider norms through this argument, and we have the following. The norms that accompany white domination are particular. Addressing broader possibilities of norms means an ever-expanding normative world. Let us keep that thought for further analysis.

The colonization of our planetary space also had with it the colonization of time. Time was divided after the 15th century into a Eurocentered
one, which was presumed to be the present into the future. That juncture
produced "primitive" or "premodern" time, which was marked from then
onward as belonging to "the past." Such a past was not merely descriptive.
It was also *normative* in the sense of a moment that deserved not only to
become past but also preferably *primordially past*—as distant a past as possible.
The anthropological result was, as we have seen, ultimately two types of
people—Euromodern and the supposedly premodern rest. As with the first
stage of double consciousness, Euromodern consciousness presumed itself
simply to be "modern." It thus had another premise. To become modern,
others must become European or at least European-like. The norms, premised on European normativity, then followed.

The Anglo-American philosopher John Rawls famously argued that justice is the primary virtue of social institutions.[18] He gave no argument for
this. He simply asserted it as a given. But what if justice were not the primary
virtue but instead simply *a* virtue (among others) for societal institutions?
Would there not be more to learn?

This question is central also for the understanding of an important institution: law. It would put us astray to go through debates on legal positiv-
ism, hermeneutical legal theory, pragmatic legal theory, deontological legal
theory, varieties of rules and regulation, and sovereignty and other forms of
ultimate purposes of law.[19] What I should simply like us to observe is that
laws are expected to be just. If laws are colonized, then our presumption is
that they are subordinated to a set of norms that, while offering authority,
may not offer justice. This misses the larger point of the colonization of
institutions and, even more, the conceptual frameworks through which they
become meaningful. It could very well be that the only justice that could be
offered by any legal system will be in terms of its models of authority. The
achievement of justice could, in other words, be an unjust situation for many
people. Even worse, the fight against that injustice could lead to practices
of justice presumed endless in their scope. If the norms of justice were the
problem to begin with, simply expanding their membership may be the per-
petuation of their damage.

What Rawls and many others presumed was at least a universal adherence
to having a concept of justice in every human society. Thus, many commen-
tators, translators, and he simply expected to find equivalent terms across
societies and simply bring them in stream with their argument.[20] Rawls was
more careful than most. He added the proviso of a "well-ordered society"
and claimed that his argument depended on the "basic structure" of the one
in which he (as the theorist) lived. Thus, he distinguished between *his theory*,
which he called "justice as fairness," also announced as "*a* theory of justice,"
from justice itself. In effect, he was showing "justice *for*" or what "justice is"
in Anglo-American society, which led to debates between his followers

and him on the question of his theory's scope, as some have argued for its *global application.*[21]

A problem with his position was Rawls's philosophical anthropological and cultural understanding of "American society." As Jane Anna Gordon and Michael Monahan have shown, drawing as well on research across the human sciences, there is no such thing as a genuinely homogeneous society.[22] There is simply the struggle *for* purity through which such models are offered. Rawls's "Anglo-American society" (pluralistic only in its members' diverse interests or notions of the good) was already a distortion. The only case he could ultimately build for basing his thought on such a cultural fiction was the power invested in it, which, in sum, relied on white Anglo-Saxon and Protestant exemplars and their intellectual descendants from Europe.[23]

Jane Anna Gordon's argument about the creolization of political theory connects to a concern of epistemic decolonization that addresses colonialization even at methodological levels. Appeals to "pure" human populations and normatively "pure" societies often accompany presuppositions of disciplinary and methodological purity. In other words, as Michael Monahan has argued alongside her, political purity and methodological purity converge. This quest for purity, I have argued in *Disciplinary Decadence*, turns disciplines away from reality in their quest for controlled outcomes.[24] Reality becomes problematic, in other words, because it is, quite simply, "impure" and resistant to complete control.[25] Put differently, as Karl Jaspers argued, it is simply always bigger than we are and, thus, ultimately, outside of our domain and control.[26]

I call this phenomenon of organized, reality-ignoring epistemic practices "disciplinary decadence." It occurs when a discipline gives up its reach for or at least movement toward reality and turns inward to make itself into reality. It, thus, treats its methods as practices created by the equivalent of gods. "Fetishizing" of method emerges. This problem occurs in many disciplines, including those among the avowed natural sciences. It often goes unnoticed until the discipline's zombified status is revealed through its eventually going, in a word, nowhere. There are many past disciplines that suffered this fate. Think of alchemy and phrenology. To some extent, what is today called "moral philosophy" is already showing signs of such decay, especially as some of its most vociferous proponents are among the most unethical people I have encountered in the academy. Their names are not mentioned here for the obvious distraction that would initiate from the larger argument. Psychoanalysis would no doubt offer much illumination on that issue.

A clear example of disciplinary decadence is moral philosophy's relationship to political philosophy in what is considered "mainstream" philosophy, whether analytical or Eurocontinental. A criticism of John Rawls's *A Theory of Justice* is that it is hailed as a work of political philosophy when it is, in fact, one of moral philosophy. Rawls presumed that, as a liberal theory, the issue was to demonstrate the right way to organize society according to principles best suited for regulating its basic institutions. He presumed these principles, including the ideological rationalization supporting them—namely, liberalism—could exist *independently* of the historical activities and theories that formed Euromodern society such as conquest, colonialism, genocide, racism, and the philosophical anthropology of egoistic self-interest that supported arrangements premised on market exploitation. It did not occur to him that the values for which he was arguing could have been *produced* by such arrangements mainly because he worked within a methodologically presumed premise of normative and egological independence. The circularity inherent in the appeal to the completely separated but reflective rational agent comes to the fore here. Why did all this amount to a moral instead of political philosophy? It was *the rules* to which Rawls was ultimately appealing. In other words, his effort was to subordinate politics to rule, which, in effect, revealed a misunderstanding of the former.

Rawls later defended his position *as political* in *Justice as Fairness: A Restatement*.[27] Interestingly enough, a feature of his earlier effort fell to the wayside. His contractarian theory appealing to such notions as an "overlapping consensus" resulting from reflection ("reflective equilibrium") pointed toward Jean-Jacques Rousseau's concept of a general will (versus a will in general) as the exemplification of sovereignty in *The Social Contract* (1762).[28] The will in general refers to a collection of individual interests; the general will addresses what it would be unreasonable to reject. Yet in his restatement, Rawls argued that his theory was political because it ultimately addressed the regulation of power. When he defined power, however, it was not Rousseau to whom he appealed but instead to Thomas Hobbes's notion of power as fundamentally coercive. Hobbes, in his *Leviathan* (1651), subscribed to this view because of his atomistic philosophical anthropology and bleak portrait of human nature, which did not regard human beings as relationships with each other but instead as on a collision course properly averted through the intervening force of a mighty entity. The supervening force of regulation (the principles) for Rawls thus becomes the deciding factor, which, in effect, makes rule supervene over politics. Interestingly enough, the ancients with whom adherents of such forms of political theory or philosophy claimed affinity, had a disparaging term for an individual who subordinated political life: namely, ἰδιώτης (*idiōtēs*), *a private person, one not concerned with public affairs—in short, an idiot.*[29]

Fanon, whose intellectual genealogy included not only Afro-Caribbean philosophical anthropological conceptions of health by way of Aimé Césaire and other Africana intellectuals (a purely rational mind is not a human one) but also Rousseau's general will, saw otherwise.[30] The moral regulation of political institutions presumed the legitimacy of the moral norms in the first place. Euromodern colonialism and its concomitant racism placed a conundrum on this normative, liberal effort: the norms could only work if there were changes put into place. But how could those changes occur through the deployment of norms that were at home under the dehumanizing status quo? In other words, different conditions were necessary paradoxically for the emergence of such norms *as legitimate*. Put differently, political action was needed for the sake of establishing ethical relations even for the legitimacy of moral norms. A consequence of colonialism is, thus, a call for this: politics supervenes.

The question that follows is what exactly is *politics*? We already see that power (from Latin *potis*, which was, in turn, from Middle Kingdom Mdw Ntr *pHty*, godlike strength) plays an important role. Politics itself emerges under different names throughout the history of our species, but the one occasioning this nomenclature is from the Greek word *pólis*, which referred to ancient Hellenic city-states. Imagine a wall or barrier or border surrounding such a state in which conflict is handled in different ways *inside* versus *outside*. Inside, conflicts are negotiated through speech, wherein power is the ability to affect the social world. The "reach" of the participants, in other words, is potentially across the entire society, but their conduct must be without coercion.[31] It is, thus, already antipathetic to the Hobbesian model. Outside, there is another story. There, the physical force could be used, where the proper word, depending on the groups of agents involved, would be "war," an activity governed by, as Suárez-Krabbe correctly reminded us, drawing on the description used by the Mamos (Indigenous juridical custodians of Mother Earth in Abya Yala), "the death project."[32] If such force is used inside, its justification could only be that the rules of discursive negotiation—speech—have been breached and that the welfare of the city-state is threatened. If what is proper "outside" is brought "inside," the reality is civil war (that is, the city-state at war with itself), a condition in which death instead of life dominates.

There are ways in which Hobbes could defend his position in the model outlined here. Others, such as Hannah Arendt, Jean-Paul Sartre, Fanon, and even Rawls's colleague Amartya Sen, would point out that the central difference would be in the conception of power at work.[33] Power need not be exclusively coercive. There is also enabling power, if by power we mean the ability to make things happen, to make the possible actual. This positive idea of power, often characterized as *empowerment*, is part of the mythological life of our species. It is, in its metaphysical form, as the ancient Kmt formulation makes clear, what the gods offer. By protecting us against the elements, malediction, and infelicitous aims of our fellow human beings, they enable us to focus on activities conducive to flourishing. The three protective elements could be reformulated as necessary resources (food, water, and shelter), health, and laws. In some cases, we ask the gods for the addition of luck or blessedness (a better translation of the ancient Greek word *eudaimonia*, in my view), but in all, the idea is for human beings to access a life that would be otherwise miserable. Extract the gods from this equation, and we find that human beings have been able to develop these conditions through culture, which Sigmund Freud, we should remember, astutely called a "prosthetic god."[34] This "god" offers institutions through which such services could be addressed, and the concentration of power through which the many institutions are regulated and administered is, in a word, *government*.

What is legitimate in placing such investments in government or institutions of rule? Although physical force could be rallied through rule, what ultimately make this possible are social conditions through which an order could translate into an action a great distance away from its source. In other words, the social world as the expansion of meaning is also what enables power beyond individual brute strength to occur, to make things happen. The source of all this is people, and here the circumstance shifts as the basis of such power becomes their investments—their willingness, in effect—for power to consolidate in institutions and the individuals who represent them. We could call this "legitimacy."

Where governing or ruling forces fail to offer the services of the prosthetic god, the subjects face the problem of their divestment of power without returns. And in fact, the ruling institutions eventually maintain force, which descends into violence, instead of power as their subjects increasingly divest themselves from a world of avowed investments with a lack of returns. In other words, the cart is placed before the horse, where the people become servants of the governing institutions instead of the latter providing services for the common weal. For our purposes, the elimination of a voice in the negotiation of power, which is an effect of eroding legitimation, entails a situation of rendering speech irrelevant to the mechanisms and practices of power (making things happen). But at this point, things continue to happen for whose benefit or purpose? If the proverbial "people" become irrelevant, how, then, could politics—the negotiation and distribution of power across the social world—remain possible? The supervenience of rule marks the end of politics. This, then, is the problem with the rule- or principles-first model of political philosophy and political theory: it requires the elimination of politics (in favor of moral rule) and is, thus, patently *not* an exemplification of political thought. It is, simply, morality being offered as sovereign over social reality.

For our purposes, the problem takes a peculiar form when we consider it as one field of philosophy supervening over another as the legitimating condition of what the other was originally proposed to address. It is, in short, a form of disciplinary decadence. In effect, political philosophy *as political philosophy* is rendered illegitimate in liberal political thought because of the prioritizing of moral philosophy. Political life could only enter the discourse as legitimate, in other words, as ethics or moral philosophy. How is this overcome?

One overcomes disciplinary decadence by pushing methodological fetishism and disciplinary nationalism to the side for the sake of reality. This act, which I call a "teleological suspension of disciplinarity," involves, as what Jane Anna Gordon, building on ideas from W.E.B. Du Bois and Paget Henry, calls "potentiated double consciousness," a constant establishing of relationships toward a reality that always exceeds us. We learn *more* but not *all*. In this case, it means taking seriously important elements of politics when addressing political problems. As part of the human world, political problems are contingent but not accidental. They require being attuned to the evidential ways in which human beings build and offer meaning to the social world in which human activities are manifested. This means also addressing ways in which that world also sometimes hides from itself. Bad faith, the form of self-lie in which the liar evades displeasing truths in favor of pleasing falsehoods, is another way of describing disciplinary decadence, where the practitioner hides from the displeasing reality of disciplinary limitation through appealing to the lie of methodological completeness. The teleological suspension of disciplinarity is an admission of incompleteness. This avowal entails paying attention to the evidential features of reality, bringing critical insight to bear on norms at hand. This means addressing the increasing capabilities of the human world and, in so doing, taking a position toward making things happen—power—as a responsibility of actively building instead of imposing meanings, agreements, and rules as negotiations of power. Instead of an epistemological condition of prior knowledge, there is, instead, the creative one of discovery as an activity of living relations with times and circumstances to which such thought is indigenous.

Now, what is curious is that although many critics would agree about transcending knowledge claims of hubristic disciplines and orientations to thought, many in my experience are reluctant to do such regarding normative ones. Epistemic decolonization is fine, but for many, the idea of transcending justice is, in a word, terrifying.

A teleological suspension of a discipline is not, I would like to add, the elimination of that discipline. The similarity of this argument to Søren Kierkegaard's about teleological suspensions of ethics in *Frygt og Bœven* ("Fear and Trembling") is not accidental. Recall that Kierkegaard argued that the ability to leap beyond the universal (morality) for the Absolute (reality for the secular, the great deity for others) can also be an ethical act of taking responsibility for transcending such forms of responsibility. It is, in other words, an existential paradox. What emerges is a different relationship to ethical life, though he also shows that it could also be a relationship with demonic existence, too. In doing such with regard to disciplines it could mean the production of new kinds or even that which is beyond disciplines. It could also mean catastrophic failure. Similarly, it may be the case that justice has a particular scope but what humanity demands is beyond the range of justice. We could think of justice beyond justice, but problems today may demand something more radical, given the reflections of political reality supervening over morality at least as offered by the Euromodern world.

The Euromodern colonial world assaulted human dignity, freedom, and much of our species' ways of understanding reality. Addressing these require theorizing anthropology (what is a human being and how is such study possible?), freedom and liberation (what shall we become?), and all justificatory practices. For the sake of brevity, I will not spell out the details of this triumvirate here, as I have already mentioned exploring its various dynamics elsewhere.[35]

Here is a problem of justice that brings all these together. Every effort simply to bring people of color, especially black people, "into" the sphere of Euromodern justice has led to double standards. This is because for most of the rules to work, the humanity of those subjected to them must be admitted and adhered to. That this factor is absent in many Euromodern attempts at justice is evident. There simply is more justice for white people in practice than there are for other groups as global inequalities and institutional responses to matters of life and death demonstrate. It makes many whites uncomfortable to hear this. It may even make some ashamed. But it is true by virtue of the facts. There is much social scientific evidence that whites are rarely punished for major crimes, whereas blacks and other racialized minorities are severely punished even for minor ones, and even worse, there are many punished for crimes they did not actually commit.[36] This in no way disrupts the moral conscience of the contemporary dominating normative systems across the globe, although there are growing activist movements fighting for otherwise.[37]

What this tells us is not that societies should now equalize things by simply punishing everyone for minor offenses and even incarcerating many across racial lines who have not committed crimes. It does tell us that we simply treat people differently the extent to which we take their humanity seriously. That many whites do commit offenses without punishment raises important questions about whether many illicit activities are as detrimental to public welfare as suggested by their illegality.[38] Put differently, their enforcement may simply be a form of unjust justice.

Although I am raising this problem at the heart of the normative force of Euromodern conceptions of justice, it is ironically also there in the appearance of a popular theory such as Rawls's in the historical record. Charles Houston, the famed African American civil rights jurist and former Dean of Howard University Law School, had formulated what are now known as Rawls's two principles of justice a little more than two decades before Rawls but argued for a different outcome where the two principles conflict.[39] Rawls, as is well known, argued that justice in the United States should be ordered according to two principles—one that prioritizes civil liberties and another that responds to inequalities and disadvantages. The latter, he contended, is fair if inequalities actually benefit the least advantaged members of the society. If there were a situation in which these principles were in conflict, Rawls advocated prioritizing the first principle over the second. In other words, civil liberties, which Rawls regarded as necessary conditions for the formation of moral persons, must be protected even at the expense of the least advantaged people.

Houston, however, argued that where the two principles conflict, it is the difference principle that should prevail.[40] He argued for the material transformation of inequalities over the prioritizing of liberties because action requires material conditions of possibility; liberties on which one cannot act are empty. He in effect questioned the formation of the moral person outside of a materially significant framework of social reflection. His criticism of Rawls would in effect be that Rawls argued as though a principle could serve as both necessary and sufficient conditions for its manifestation. Although that clearly was not Rawls's intent given his overall aspiration for a decent society, which for him—and he presumed most if not the rest of us—meant a just social order.

We see here different positions on a fundamentally human question. Because Rawls writes from a perspective that imagines the capacity to create material conditions so long as liberty is maintained, his heuristic model is much like that of the once-imagined Robinson Crusoe. No doubt Rawls belongs to the community of readers who identify with *Crusoe*. What Houston—and many black and Indigenous peoples—knew was that the Crusoe model is fallacious precisely because it posits the other human being on the island, the character Friday, *outside of society*, when the question at hand is about building a just society, which, in the case of Daniel Defoe's novel, was the island. Crusoe relied on Friday, whose rejected humanity in the narrative facilitated Crusoe's delusions of self-sufficiency. That the problem already presupposes a world of others—or at least in the novel's case, one other—entails that the inherent sociality of social conditions has to be taken into account.

The Dalit intellectual V.T. Rajshekar formulates this problem of structured exclusion this way in *Dalit: The Black Untouchables of India*.[41] The error is in the trap of assimilation as an expectation of integration. The latter involves placing people under the jurisdiction of a hegemonic group whose norms of belonging depend on exclusion or, even more radical, untouchability of the subordinated group. Brahmins, for example, took control over people in the Indian subcontinent and other parts of South Asia at the departure of the British. Their condition of legitimate membership depended on the people under their jurisdiction being designated as Hindus, even though many of the people, especially the many groups linked to the ancient, dark-skin Indigenous peoples, rejected Hinduism because of its commitment to their exclusion. To "belong" to Hinduism entailed them being "untouchable." Their appearance would be, in a word, illicit. For some groups, even their shadows constitute "pollution." Implementing Brahminic models of justice, then, offers them no hope. Many Dalits, then, are paradoxically assimilated into Hinduism as unassimilable. Assimilation promised along with their integration is, for them, a nightmare.

Returning to Houston and Rawls, we also see a crucial difference between portraits of the human being as a substance in isolation versus a relationship that presupposes a world of others and in which struggle is required for things that really matter. This is one reason why, despite their shared concerns for a just society, Houston's and Rawls's intellectual and political paths point to different directions. Houston's places him with revolutionary thinkers on law and society while Rawls's theory points to reforms of a society that is presumed to be basically decent. Houston was well aware of how indecent U.S. society was, and many continue to see as of the writing of this chapter, toward blacks, Indigenous, and varieties of racialized and poor peoples. The ideas of Houston and Rawls are premised on fundamentally different philosophical anthropologies. The relationality of the human being for Houston is, in other words, the task through which not only justice must be cultivated but also the human being (and human wellbeing) should come to the fore without compromise. Rajshekar would agree with him.

Houston and Rajshekar would regard Rawls as advocating an unjust justice. Rawls would, at least with regard to the difference principle, regard them as advancing injustice.

There is another consideration if we are willing to go beyond the formal constraints posed by such principles, though I suspect, at least from the perspective of decolonization, Houston and Rajshekar would prevail if justice were the aim beyond which we were unwilling to go.

The human question must have normative force beyond formal conceptions of justice. Being humane, for instance, may mean looking at justice as limited if made maximally consistent. Consistency requires no contradictions, and maximum consistency requires no exceptions. But I suspect most, if not all, human beings (except for perhaps sociopaths) consider such an approach unreasonable. That to be reasonable means being willing to transcend the maximally consistent practice of rules—in other words, being willing to break a rule or at least find an exemption to it—brings the point to the fore; it may be in the interest of a greater set of norms to pose the limits of another set.

An astute logician might simply place in the set of meta-rules *this rule of exception* to render the overall system consistent. Many readers would see the flaws here. It will simply be an admission of exception, which, paradoxically, would be an exception that is not an exception. In other words, a *real exception* would require breaking the rule of the system, including its rule of consistency.

I would like to submit here that there might be norms more attuned to a world attempting to transcend colonialism and racism than those handed down from the colonial system—that is, an order premised on a philosophical anthropology indigenous to such forms of oppression. These alternative norms emerged from a basic, practical consideration. Consider that the norms different communities developed in the precolonial periods did not disappear at the moment of colonization. As ways of organizing life, they were drawn upon to assess the new situation of being in relations with those who colonized them. Colonialism is, in this view, not the erasure of agency of colonized peoples. It is *the attempted erasure*. What happens is the ongoing development of norms premised on identifying and being critical of the wrongs of the new system. These are potentiated double-conscious norms. They are norms attuned to the limitations of the system, and they do so through the intercommunicative or creolized practices of normative production. If this is correct, then it means so-called indigenous normative systems are, in fact, modern through-and-through. And even more, they are not *Euro*modern as they are aware of the *particularity* of Euromodernity. They could see, for example, that they are not a subspecies of, say, "justice," whose etymology and genealogy are from Latin, but something more through which justice is perhaps a subspecies.

The argument advanced here is premised on the human being as *a relational being*. In effect, this means one cannot place a formerly excluded human being into a context without changing its relations. To do otherwise would be to erase the relations by which that new participant manifested and impose upon her or him an external set of relations whose effect is the maintenance of the given order or system. Changing the relations sets the framework for the production of different relations. In effect, we are speaking here of a teleological suspension of humanity as currently conceived—the human being beyond currently hegemonic modes of being human.

Justice, then, as a relation premised on a specific philosophical anthropology, works the extent to which one is committed to that anthropology. To expand the normative reach of human reality holds within it the transformation of that reality, which means, as well, the transformation of different norms. Attempts to squeeze this expanded human being (here interpreted as fundamentally incomplete) into a previously closed conception of the human being produce a peculiar form of suffering. When the closed system is justice, it is an unusual agony—*miserable justice*.

The great East Indian philosopher Sri Aurobindo offers this reflection, which brings these considerations to the fore:

> … absolute love, absolute justice, absolute right reason in their present application by a bewildered and imperfect humanity come easily to be conflicting principles. Justice often demands what love abhors. Right reason dispassionately considering the facts of nature and human relations in search of a satisfying norm or rule is unable to admit without modification either any reign of absolute justice or any reign of absolute love. And, in fact, man's absolute justice easily turns out to be in practice a sovereign injustice; for his mind, one-sided and rigid in its constructions, puts forward a one-sided partial and rigorous scheme or figure and claims for its totality and absoluteness and an application that ignores the subtler truth of things and the plasticity of life. All our standards turned into action either waver on a flux of compromises or err by this partiality and unelastic structure. Humanity sways from one orientation to another; the race moves upon a zigzag path led by conflicting claims and, on the whole, works out instinctively what Nature intends, but with

much waste and suffering, rather than either what it desires or what it holds to be right or what the highest light from above demands from the embodied spirit.[42]

As justice cannot alleviate this misery of a closed humanity—in fact, it is at times its goal to produce it, to make those supposedly intrinsically unjust in the system suffer—perhaps other normative possibilities for the governing of social institutions is needed. I do think that human potential is such that the symbolic ordering of social reality could be expanded. We are already seeing this as humanity struggles today to preserve certain norms while witnessing them being overcome, as Jane Anna Gordon and I have argued elsewhere.[43] This is because the older norms may have been foundational for a world in which they could no longer live.

These reflections in a way actually raise an additional consideration. It is also about *why* justice is not enough. If we return to Fanon, we see the basic problem with renewed clarity. Conceptions of political philosophy premised on bringing moral philosophy to bear on politics confuse the two. Fanon's consideration was about what must be done if there is the dilemma of maintaining the violence of an unjust system offered as justice through avowed nonviolence or fighting that system and simply accepts being constructed as unjust and violent. As violence, or, better, violation, is in both directions, the problem is not *morally* resolved. Even worse, its moral irresolution depends on a structured inequality of power. Thus, Fanon argued that colonialism has, in fact, derailed the project of a moral grounding of political life. Instead, the question of the political action for the emergence of different normative relations is needed. This is why justice is not enough; politics, actual political action, is, as we have seen, needed without the advanced guarantee of what is "right." This is the existential situation. When justice is not enough, political action is needed for the normative conditions of value that may transcend justice—and it may do so for the sake of something not immediately apparent such as a set of relations *better than justice*.

Justice may actually be a particular conception of institutional virtue instead of, as Rawls and theorists of liberal political thought claimed, *the* primary virtue of social institutions.[44] Much of this emerges from the presumed translatability of justice as completely isomorphic with the norms of non-Western societies—or, worse, so valuable that if it is not part of the norms of those societies, it should be *imposed upon them*. Where there is a breakdown, the presumption has been that justice is the broader, because presumably more universal, term. But what if justice is a particular term and the other terms, such as "*Ubuntu*" in South Africa or even "*MAat*," signified by the delicate balancing challenge of the feather "β" of the ancient Kmt goddess that is its namesake, are of broader scope and normative significance?[45] This would mean that justice, though an important, perhaps necessary, value to defend, is an insufficient condition of what may be needed in the organization of institutions in societies seeking to move past colonialism and racism. If justice is insufficient, what, then, are the normative resources to which we should appeal? We have already seen some of the paradoxes of the hegemony of justice leading to forms of unjust justice. Could a just justice be a normative ideal *beyond justice*? How do "we," by whom I mean those of us nurtured on the hegemony of justice, even make this move?

Insight on these questions emerges from a critique of isomorphism and translation. Both presuppose completeness of Western normative life— namely, that the domain of normative possibilities is already encompassed by Western epistemic practices. A way of thinking otherwise has been offered by the Ghanaian philosopher Kwasi Wiredu, who argued for the expansion of epistemic and normative life through appealing to our already-given capacity to communicate across different languages and learn new words, new concepts, and, I here insist, develop new values.[46] In other words, just as we could learn new ideas, we could also develop new norms. There is much evidence for this that in the varieties of ways we are relating to each other in the world today as new *kinds* of human beings emerge, especially regarding sexual orientation and technologies of embodiment. The emergence of new modes of living raises questions of expanding our normative capacities. The task now, at least in terms of normative thought, is to face that challenge, expand our concepts and build new sets of normative relations attuned to a world where justice is, in the end, not enough.

Notes

1. James Boggs, *Pages from a Black Radical's Notebook: A James Boggs Reader*, Stephen M. Ward (ed.) (Detroit, MI: Wayne State University Press, 2011), 85.
2. The students' movement across South Africa early in the second decade of the new millennium, with declarations of "fees must fall" and decolonizing universities, which spilled out over the globe by 2015, makes this clear. For discussion of this movement, which is sometimes call "falllism," see A. Kayhum Ahmed, "The Rise of Fallism: #RhodesMustFall and the Movement to Decolonize the University" (Columbia University Doctoral Thesis in Comparative and International Education, 2019) and "On Black Pain/Black Liberation and the Rise of Fallism," *Black Issues in Philosophy* (19 March 2019): https://blog.apaonline.org/2019/03/19/on-black-pain-black-liberation-and-the-rise-of-fallism/.
3. I am, of course, referring to Frantz Fanon's classic *Les Damnés de la terre* (Paris: Éditions Gallimard, 1991 [1961]). Again, as translations are mine, I simply refer to this work as *The Damned of the Earth*. I elaborate the short summary offered here in *What Fanon Said: A Philosophical Introduction to His Life and Thought* (New York, NY: Fordham UP; London, UK: Hurst; Johannesburg, South Africa: Wits University Press, 2015).
4. In addition to the already cited writings in Chapters 1 and 2 by Sayan Dey, Quijano, Maldonado-Torres, Mignolo, Sanín-Restrepo, and Walsh, see María Lugones, "The Coloniality of Gender," *World Knowledges Otherwise* 2, no. 2 (2008): 1–17 and "Towards a Decolonial Feminism," *Hypatia* 25, no. 4 (Fall, 2010): 742–759.

5. See, e.g., Quobna Ottobah Cugoano, *"Thoughts and Sentiments on the Evil of Slavery" and Other Writings* (New York, NY: Penguin Books, 1999). For discussion of others, also in the 19th century, see Lewis R. Gordon, *An Introduction to Africana Philosophy*, 2nd Edition (Cambridge, UK: Cambridge University Press, 2021).
6. Bartolomé de Las Casas, *Short Account of the Destruction of the Indies*, trans. by Nigel Griffin (New York, NY: Penguin Classics, 1999).
7. Nelson Maldonado-Torres, "On the Coloniality of Being: Contributions to the Development of a Concept," *Cultural Studies* 21, nos. 2–3 (2007): 240–270.
8. In addition to Quijano, Maldonado-Torres, and Suárez-Krabbe, see Walter Mignolo, "The Geopolitics of Knowledge and the Colonial Difference," *The South Atlantic Quarterly* 101, no. 1 (2002): 57–96; *The Darker Side of Western Modernity: Global Futures, Decolonial Options* (Durham, NC: Duke University Press, 2011), and Walter Mignolo and Catherine Walsh, *On Decoloniality: Concepts, Analytics, Praxis* (Durham, NC: Duke University Press, 2018). See also Lewis R. Gordon, *Existentia Africana: An Introduction to African Existential Thought* (New York, NY: Routledge, 2000).
9. See Nelson Maldonado-Torres, *Against War: Views from the Underside of Modernity* (Durham, NC: Duke University Press, 2008) and "Thinking through the Decolonial Turn: Post-continental Interventions in Theory, Philosophy, and Critique—An Introduction," *Transmodernity* 1, no. 2 (Fall 2011): 1–15; Boaventura de Sousa Santos, *Epistemologies of the South: Justice against Epistemicide* (New York, NY: Routledge, 2014) and *The End of the Cognitive Empire: The Coming of Age of Epistemologies of the South* (Durham, NC: Duke University Press, 2018); Catherine Walsh, "The Decolonial *For*: Resurgences, Shifts, and Movements," in Walter Mignolo and Catherine Walsh, *On Decoloniality*, 15–32; Julia Suàrez-Krabbe, *Race, Rights and Rebels: Alternatives beyond Human Rights and Development* (London, UK: Rowman & Littlefield International, 2015); and Ricardo Sanín-Restrepo, *Decolonizing Democracy* (London, UK; Rowman & Littlefield International, 2016).
10. This is no doubt on the minds of many as the most volatile exemplars of hate and theft ascended to the chief executive office of countries ranging from Brazil, India, and the United Kingdom to the United States near the end of the second decade of the 20th century, but we should bear in mind that the seeds were sown long ago. We should think as well of how this question of morality versus intelligence played out in the financial sector. See, e.g., David Enrich, *Dark Towers: Deutsche Bank, Donald Trump, and an Epic Trial of Destruction* (New York, NY: HarperCollins, 2020). Mogobe Ramose offers a genealogy of normative bases of this phenomenon at the heart of Christian rationalizations of conquest and colonization in "Justice and Restitution in African Political Thought," in P.H. Coetzee and A.P. J. Rous (eds.), *The African Philosophy Reader: A Text with Readings*, 2nd Edition (London, UK: Routledge, 2003), see 541–553.
11. Frantz Fanon, *Peau noire, masques blancs* (Paris, France: Éditions du Seuil, 1952), known in English as *Black Skin, White Masks*, Chapter 7. See my discussion in Gordon, *What Fanon Said*. Although seemingly unaware of Fanon's and the long line of African diasporic thinkers' views on this subject, David Livingstone Smith also articulates a similar view in *Less Than Human: Why We Demean, Enslave, and Exterminate Others* (New York: St. Martin's Press, 2011).
12. See, for example, Martin Buber's classic analysis of his relationship to a tree in *I and Thou*, trans. *Ronald Gregor Smith* (Mansfield, CT: Martin Publishing, 2010 [1923]), 7–10.
13. See Immanuel Kant, *Groundwork for the Metaphysics of Morals*, trans. Mary Gregor and Jens Timmermann (Cambridge, UK: Cambridge University Press, 2012) and *Critique of Practical Reason*, trans. Werner S. Pluhar (Indianapolis, IN: Hackett, 2002).

14. Emprical studies of institutionally produced white wealth and black poverty are many. Here are a few: Claude Anderson, *Black Labor, White Wealth: The Search for Power and Economic Justice* (Bethesda, MD: PowerNomics Corporation of America, 1994); Melvin Oliver and Thomas Shapiro (eds.), *Black Wealth / White Wealth: A New Perspective on Racial Inequality*, 2nd Edition (New York, NY: Routledge, 2006); Ira Katznelson, *When Affirmative Action Was White: An Untold History of Racial Inequality in Twentieth-Century America* (New York, NY: W.W. Norton, 2005); Shawn D. Rochester, *The Black Tax: The Cost of Being Black in America* (Southbury, CT: Good Steward Publishing, 2017); Mehrsa Baradaran, *The Color of Money: Black Banks and the Racial Wealth Gap* (Cambridge, MA: Harvard University Press, 2017). Most of these discussions focus on the United States despite the global racial impact of Euromodern colonialism; for a global example, see Walter Rodney, *How Europe Underdeveloped Africa* (Washington, DC: Howard University Press, 1982).

15. This concept points to W.E.B. Du Bois, although he did not quite formulate it this way. Paget Henry offers the concept of "potentiated second sight" in his "Africana Phenomenology: Its Philosophical Implications," in Paget Henry, Jane Anna Gordon, Lewis R. Gordon, Aaron Kamugisha, and Neil Roberts (eds.), *Journeys in Caribbean Thought: The Paget Henry Reader* (London, UK: Rowman & Littlefield International, 2016), 27–58; Jane Anna Gordon offers the formulation referenced here in her chapter "The General Will as Political Legitimacy: Disenchantment and Double Consciousness in Modern Democratic Life" (Philadelphia,PA: University of Pennsylvania Doctoral Dissertation in Political Science, 2005), "The Gift of Double Consciousness: Some Obstacles to Grasping the Contributions of the Colonized," in Nalini Persram (ed.), *Postcolonialism and Political Theory* (Lanham, MD: Lexington Books, 2007), 143–161, and *Creolizing Political Theory: Reading Rousseau through Fanon* (New York, NY: Fordham University Press, 2014). I offer discussion of varieties of double consciousness in many of my writings, but see *An Introduction to Africana Philosophy* for summaries. There is also the concept of doubled double consciousness in Nahum Dimitri Chandler, *X—The Problem of the Negro as a Problem for Thought* (New York, NY: Fordham University Press, 2014).

16. For elaboration of the Euromodern love affair with animals and its connection to racism, see Bénédicte Boisseron, *Afro-Dog: Blackness and the Animal Question* (New York, NY: Columbia University Press, 2018) and Lewis R. Gordon, *Fear of Black Consciousness* (New York, NY: Farrar, Giroux & Strauss; London, UK: Penguin Books, 2021).

17. See Kimberlé Crenshaw, "Mapping the Margins: Intersectionality, Identity Politics, and Violence Against Women of Color," *Stanford Law Review* 43 (July, 1991): 1241–1299 and, interviewed by Bim Adewunmi, "Kimberlé Crenshaw on Intersectionality: 'I wanted to come up with an everyday metaphor that anyone could use," *The New Statesman* (2 April 2014): http://www.newstatesman.com/lifestyle/2014/04/kimberl-crenshaw-intersectionality-i-wanted-come-everyday-metaphor-anyone-could. Crenshaw also adds a phenomenology of lived experience of harm. For a feminist analysis that is intersectional and attuned to Marxist critiques from the context of African struggles for revolutionary social change and addressing gender-based violence, see Lynn Ossome, *Gender, Ethnicity, and Violence in Kenya's Transitions to Democracy: States of Violence* (Lanham, MD: Lexington Books, 2018).

18. John Rawls, *A Theory of Justice* (Cambridge, MA: Harvard University Press, 1971).

19. Ronald Dworkin offers an excellent outline of these approaches in his classic study *Law's Empire* (Cambridge, MA: The Belknap Press, 1986).

20. See, e.g., N. Daniels (ed.), *Reading Rawls: Critical Studies of Rawls' "A Theory of Justice"* (Palo Alto, CA: Stanford University Press, 1989).

21. The leading proponent of global application of the theory is his now ignominious student Thomas Pogge, *World Poverty and Human Rights: Cosmopolitan Responsibilities and Reform*, 2nd Edition (Cambridge, UK: Polity, 2008). For critical discussion of this debate from an African's perspective, see Chika Mba, "Fanon's Cultural Humanism and the Challenge of Global Justice" (PhD Dissertation in Philosophy, University of Ibadan, 2015).

22. Jane Anna Gordon, *Creolizing Political Theory* and Michael J. Monahan, *The Creolizing Subject: Race, Reason, and the Politics of Purity* (New York, NY: Fordham University Press, 2011). See also Rawls's student Michelle Moddy-Adams's thought-provoking book *Fieldwork in Familiar Places: Morality, Culture, & Philosophy* (Cambridge, MA: Harvard University Press, 1997).

23. This difference in the implementation of law is particularly stark when it comes to race. For alternative portraits in the U.S. and beyond, see Richard Rothstein, *The Color of Law: A Forgotten History of Our Government Segregated America* (New York, NY: Liveright Publishing Corporation, 2017); Noël Cazenave's *Killing African Americans: Police Vigilante Violence as a Racial control Mechanism* (New York, NY: Routledge, 2018); Jean Comaroff and John L. Comaroff, *The Truth About Crime: Sovereignty, Knowledge, Social Order* (Chicago, IL: University of Chicago Press, 2016); Michelle Alexander, *The New Jim Crow: Mass Incarceration in the Age of Colorblindness* (New York, NY: Free Press, 2010); Angela J. Davis, *Arbitrary Justice: The Power of the American Prosecutor* (New York, NY: Oxford University Press, 2009); Khalil Gibran Muhammad, *The Condemnation of Blackness: Race, Crime, and the Making of Modern urban America* (Cambridge, MA: Harvard University Press, 2011); and Michael Tillotson, *Invisible Jim Crow: Contemporary Ideological Threats to the Internal Security of African Americans* (Trenton, NJ: Africa World Press, 2011).

24. Lewis R. Gordon, *Disciplinary Decadence: Living Thought in Trying Times* (New York, NY: Routledge, 2006).

25. This is the underlying reminder of existential thought, as so many realize not only with the COVID-19 pandemic but also what emerges in each reminder of the consequences of climate change. With regard to the former, the most power articulation was Albert Camus's *The Plague*, trans. Stuart Gilbert (New York, NY: Vintage, 1991 [original, 1947]). For a wonderful summary discussion, see Alain de Botton, "Camus on the Coronavirus," *The New York Times* (19 March 2019): https://www.nytimes.com/2020/03/19/opinion/coronavirus-camus-plague.html. For an anticipatory discussion and elaboration of these themes along the broader contours of contingency and disaster, see also Jane Anna Gordon and Lewis R. Gordon, *Of Divine Warning: Reading Disaster in the Modern Age* (New York, NY: Routledge, 2009).

26. Karl Jaspers, *Existenzphilosophie* (Berlin, Germany: Walter de Gruyter, 1938). References here will be to Richard F. Grabau's translation, *Philosophy of Existence* (Philadelphia, PA: University of Pennsylvania Press, 1971) as it is a fine translation.

27. John Rawls, *Justice as Fairness: A Restatement*, ed. Erin Kelly (Cambridge, MA: Harvard University Press, 2001).

28. Compare Rawls's commentary on Rousseau not only in his aforementioned works, but also his *Lectures on the History of Political Philosophy* (Cambridge, MA: Harvard University Press, 2008).

29. We do not, of course, have to end our etymological journey in ancient Greek. I simply did so because of its hegemony among Anglo political theorists and philosophers, Rawls's primary interlocutors. Going back a few thousand years, we could examine the Middle Kingdom Egyptian word *idi* (deaf). The presumption was that a lack of hearing entailed isolation, at least in terms of audio speech.

30. See an initial connecting of Rousseau's general will and Fanon's national consciousness in *Fanon and the Crisis of European Man: An Essay in Philosophy and the Human Sciences* (New York, NY: Routledge, 1995), which Jane Anna Gordon elaborated and brought nuance to the study of contemporary thought through the lens of her appropriately titled *Creolizing Political Theory*. The second edition of *Fanon and the Crisis of European Man* (2021) includes critical essays by a group of scholars on this and related themes.

31. *The Eloquent Peasant*, 2nd Edition, trans. Loren R. Fischer (Eugene, OR: Cascade, 2015), composed in Kmt in approximately 1850 BCE, attests to the importance of speech, which, of course, make the Hellenic exemplars more recent comers on the scene.

32. See her *Race, Rights, and Rebellion*.

33. Readers surprised by the inclusion of Sen on this list should notice that "capability" is another way of saying "power" and capabilities could also refer to the project of empowerment. See Amartya Sen, *The Idea of Justice* (Cambridge, MA: Belknap Press, 2009) and for elaboration, Jane Anna Gordon (ed.), "Special Issue on Amartya Sen's the Idea of Justice," *Journal of Philosophy and Social Criticism* 40, no. 1 (January 2015): 3–89.

34. Interestingly enough, as we have seen, even the gods drew from a more radical source of power (*HqAw*, often spelled as *heka*, which refers to activating the *ka* [what facilitates all reality, sometimes translated as soul or spirit] or, in a word, "magic"), if *The Coffin Texts* (c. 2181–2055 BCE) is taken into account.

35. E.g., Lewis R. Gordon, *An Introduction to Africana Philosophy*.

36. See Noël Cazenave, *Killing African Americans*; Jean Comaroff and John L. Comaroff, *The Truth About Crime*; Michelle Alexander, *The New Jim Crow*; Angela J. Davis, *Arbitrary Justice*; Khalil Gibran Muhammad, *The Condemnation of Blackness*; and Michael Tillotson, *Invisible Jim Crow*.

37. Quite a few emerging from social media efforts such as #BlackLivesMatter.

38. Commentaries abound on this issue. See, e.g., Michelle Alexander, *The New Jim Crow*; Angela J. Davis, *Arbitrary Justice* and her edited volume *Policing the Black Man: arrest, Prosecution and imprisonment* (New York, NY: Pantheon Books, 2017); and Maya Schenwar, *Locked Down, Locked Out: Why Prions Don't Work and How We Can Do Better* (Oakland, CA: Berrett-Koehler, 2014).

39. For rich discussions of Houston's life and thought, see James Conyers, Jr. (ed.), *Charles H. Houston: An Interdisciplinary Study of Civil Rights Leadership* (Lanham, MD: Lexington Books, 2012). For Rawls, see, in addition to Daniels' *Reading Rawls*, Samuel Freeman (ed.), *The Cambridge Companion to John Rawls* (Cambridge, UK: Cambridge University Press, 2002).

40. See Charles Houston, "The Need for Negro Lawyers," *Journal of Negro Education* 4 (January 1935): 49; "Educational Inequalities Must Go," *Crisis* 42 (October 1935): 300; "Cracking Closed University Doors," *Crisis* 42 (December 1935): 364; "Glass Aided School Inequalities," *Crisis* 43 (January 1936): 15; and "Saving the World for Democracy," a series for *The Pittsburgh Courier* (July 20, 27; August 2, 17, 24, 31; September 7, 14, 21, 28; and October 5, 12, 1940). As is evident from these articles, Houston believed in getting to the point and being brief. For biography and discussion, see Rawn James, Jr., *Root and Branch: Charles Hamilton Houston, Thurgood Marshall, and the Struggle to End Segregation* (New York, NY: Bloomsbury Press, 2010) and Michael Jay Friedman, *Free At Last: The U.S. Civil Rights Movement* (Washington, DC: U.S. Dept. of State, Bureau of International Information Programs, 2008), available for free by the U.S. government at: http://www.america.gov/media/pdf/books/free-at-last.pdf#popup.

41. V.T. Rajshekar, *Dalit: The Black Untouchables of India* 3rd Edition (Atlanta, GA: Clarity Press, 2009).

42. Sri Aurobindo, *The Future Evolution of Man: The Divine Life Upon Earth* (Twin Lakes, WI: Lotus Press, 1963), 46.

43. Jane Anna Gordon and Lewis R. Gordon, *Of Divine Warning: Reading Disaster in the Modern Age* (New York, NY: Routledge, 2009).

44. Outside of the narrow set of white male philosophers who dominate this discussion in North American and European universities, there are Iris Marion Young's, Carole Pateman's, and Charles Mills's efforts. See Iris Marion Young, *Justice and the Politics of Difference* (Princeton, NJ: Princeton University Press, 2011) and Carole Pateman and Charles Mills, *Contract and Domination* (Cambridge, UK: Polity, 2007).

45. For philosophical discussion of uBuntu, see Magobe B. Ramose, *African Philosophy through Ubuntu* (Harare, ZI: Mond Books, 1999) and Mabogo More, *Looking through Philosophy in Black*. For *MAat,* see Théophile Obenga, *La Philosophie africaine de la période pharaonique: 2780–2330 avant notre ère* (Paris, France: L'Harmattan, 1990). And for recent discussion specifically in terms of law and justice, see Ato Sekyi-Otu, *Left Universalism, Africacentric Essays* (New York, NY: Routledge, 2018), and Drucilla Cornell, *Law and Revolution in South Africa: uBuntu, Dignity, and the Struggle for Constitutional Transformation* (New York, NY: Fordham University Press, 2014).

46. Kwasi Wiredu, *Cultural Universals and Particulars* (Bloomington, IN: Indiana University Press, 1996). See also Ngũgĩ wa Thiong'o's *Decolonising the Mind: the Politics of Language in African Literature* (Nairobi, Kemya: Heinemann Kenya, 1986).

Chapter 4

Teleological Suspensions for Political Life

What follows is an exploration of decadence imposed on contemporary political life and the stifling of the imagination it occasions. Much of this emerges not only from the assertion of capitalism as the age's theodicy but also its accompanying normative liberalism turned neoliberalism on the road to neoconservatism and fascism. The result is a tendency of proponents of morality taking flight into moralism at the price also of political life. What would it mean to think politically under such circumstances? For one, it involves committing a teleological suspension of epistemology through a commitment to the demands of a world that transcends the self. One must act, in other words, on the basis of what one *cannot know* and despite what one thinks one *is*.

Decadence, Disciplinary, and Otherwise

Decadence refers to a condition of decay. Each stage of decaying has its accompanying features. In human societies, these features or symptoms take the form of values and the kinds of knowledge that support them. We could call those dying values and thought. By contrast, when there is not a process of decay but instead one of growth, there are as well values and their epistemic support. We could call those living values and thought.

A symptom of a dying age is nihilism, and its epistemological consequence is the leveling of knowledge and truth often into "opinion" as evidence ceases to offer evidential affect and effect. This negative development affects disciplines—organizations and practices of producing and communicating knowledge—through making them insular. Where this occurs, practitioners of a discipline speak only to their adherents, which makes the impact of what they produce relevant only to their adherents. The discipline then collapses into epistemological solipsism. Where such thought becomes the world, then the absence of an outside creates the illusion of omniscience. The discipline becomes godlike. As such, its precepts and methodological assumptions become all its practitioners supposedly need to know. They, thus, apply those resources without expectations of external accountability. They turn away from reality and truth (beyond the precepts) because, as godlike, the discipline becomes all there is and thus all to learn. As we have seen, I call this phenomenon disciplinary decadence.

A familiar feature of our times is the tendency of practitioners of disciplines to reject ideas from other disciplines on the basis of not being their own. Readers are no doubt familiar with natural scientists who criticize practitioners of the human sciences for not being "scientific." In specific terms, biologists, chemists, and physicists, for example, may criticize historians, literary scholars, philosophers, and sociologists for not offering biological, chemical, or physical analyses. Those they criticize are not immune to this practice. There are historians who criticize others for not being historical, literary scholars who criticize others for not being literary, philosophers who do the same regarding those who are not philosophical, and sociologists for those who are not sociological. To understand this fallacy, just add "ism" to the discipline, and one has biologism, chemistryism, physicism, historicism, literary textualism, philosophicalism, and sociologism. Philosophicalism is a peculiar one here, for there is already something awry with reductivism in philosophy. It in effect makes philosophy not philosophical because so much is ignored, eliminated, or simply not seen when wholes, or what extends beyond such, are reduced to parts. To unpack that one, addressing the various approaches to philosophy reveals much.

Many Analytical philosophers, for instance, often treat analytical philosophy as philosophy *in toto*. To do so, they often reduce philosophical practice to one of its subfields such as logical analysis or epistemology governed by such argumentation. In doing so, they forget that philosophical argumentation is not always formal, and philosophical practice is not exclusively about avoiding contradictory arguments but also about demonstration and articulating insight. Their critics, mostly through Eurocontinental philosophy, often point to a lack of contextualizing in analytical argumentation. Eurocontinentalists, however, often offer textual analyses for context, and the result at times returns to a form of historical textualism in which European thought functions as the textual basis of thought itself. Critics of that position point to its Eurocentrism, but the problem is deeper, and even conservative exemplars of Eurocontinental thought have identified this problem. Such criticism there is as early as Edmund Husserl's "Philosophy as Rigorous Science," and arguably even earlier, if we take Rousseau's *Discourse on the Arts and Sciences* as an exemplar. As there was no properly European continental philosophy in Rousseau's time, Husserl is the better candidate, even though he later succumbs to the fallacy of equating European man with Reason. Others, such as Martin Heidegger, are well known for the same equivocation.

Philosophy, often overlooked, extends beyond the two contemporary dominating camps of the Euromodern academy. We could offer others, such as pragmatism, but beyond them there are philosophical practices across

Africa, Asia, and Indigenous thoughts of Australia, Abya Yala (Central and South America), and more. What all offer is a basic critical point: reducing philosophy to epistemology and logical analysis is a distortion of philosophy. Rejecting those reductions also leads to the question of what other dimensions of philosophy to reject as practitioners of the discipline reach out beyond questions of what they can know and support with formal argumentation. This includes addressing the limits of philosophy. Karl Jaspers was aware of this problem, which is why he insisted on philosophers remembering that reality is always greater than what philosophers can imagine. In doing so, he joined the ranks, though not intentionally, of non-Western philosophers such as Sri Aurobindo of India, Keiji Nishitani of Japan, Ali Shariati of Iran, and a long list of philosophers from Africa ranging from Zera Yacob of Ethiopia to V.Y. Mudimbe of the Congo and P. Mabogo More of South Africa. In all, philosophers become decadent when they lose disciplinary humility. Philosophers who understand this are willing to reach to the world and others without the approval of philosophical orthodoxies.

I devoted some extra time to philosophy in this discussion because of its clearly special place in reflections on a topic such as the quest for social change in contemporary thought. Although there are critics of philosophy, many of whom refer to themselves as "theorists," many commit the performative contradiction of doing so through the constant evocation of (mostly European) philosophers to legitimate their thought. This has been peculiarly so among poststructuralists who became prominent during the rise of the neoliberal academy. The marketability of European philosophers in a Eurocentric academy is such that their hegemony is even aided by their critics. Today this element of poststructuralist thought continues under the revitalized nomenclature of "critical theory." Different from Immanuel Kant's "critical philosophy" and the Frankfurt School's critical theory, the new form continues the poststructuralist metacritique of theory through which theory as an object of study becomes its own center in need of decentering. This movement of thought brings to the fore the initial observation of disciplinary decadence, as the tendency to turn inward and fetishize the practice's methodological assumptions return.

An aspect of disciplinary decadence to consider is its structural grammar of a theodicy. The aim of theodicy is to demonstrate the intrinsic validity of the divine through the externalizing of lived contradictions. Where the god is all-good, all-powerful, and all-knowing, it is difficult to account for the presence of life's infelicities without compromising the intrinsic goodness of a god with the power of preventing evil and injustice. In an age where legitimacy rejects theological accounts, other elements have taken the stage. Where capitalism is deified, capital as an omnipotent, omniscient, and all-good market is the substitute. This could be done with models of knowledge, such as science, or with cultural idols, such as "Western civilization." As disciplinary decadence is also a form of theodicy, so, too, are the prevailing, ultimately, decadent norms of assessing these institutions.

Capitalism, for instance, lacks any actual principle of falsification since it is premised on a purist model in which its proponents can eat their cake and have it, too. If there are crises of unemployment, environmental degradation, ill-health, and other social maledictions of scarcity or epidemiological ones such as the COVID-19 pandemic, the procapitalist response is that there is an insufficient amount of free-market directives in practice. Capitalism, thus, becomes external to causal mechanisms of such afflictions. Where there is flourishing, a strange causal potential comes in of what could occur if there were more radicalized fertile soil for capital. What, in other words, would be a sufficient or even ideal amount of investment in capital? Where capital is deified, the answer is complete privatization understood through processes of capital access. This amounts to a simple principle: *everything* is commodifiable. Or even simpler: everything and *anyone* could be bought. We are already witnessing this credo in the subversion of other institutions, including other markets too, as we have seen the fetishized and deified notion of The Market.[1] Thus, failing to think of markets other than The Market, this abstraction makes a market out of everything else; instead of knowledge of The Market, there is the market of knowledge; instead of education markets there is the market of education; instead of religious protection of sacred places from The Market, there is the market of religion; instead of political control of The Market, there is the market of politics. The list could go on, but the basic point is already evident: crucial institutions that historically controlled the scope of what is marketable have been subordinated to The Market. We could call this The Market colonization of society.[2]

Where The Market colonizes institutions of power, The Market becomes its sole exemplar. In the case of politics and knowledge, this entails The Market colonization of political life and knowledge. In the case of the latter, this involves all kinds of knowledge, including the imaginative practices of inquiry. It means, then, also The Market colonization of imagination.

Rule over Politics

Limiting political capacity and imagination involves the subordination of politics to rule. The Market, after all, in commodifying institutions stratifies their potential. This means blocking our critical capacities to think through that stratification. Take, for example, the abstraction of The Market. Elided in such an abstraction is the understanding of markets as human relations constructed through the human capacity to produce social worlds or systems, communicate them, and transform them. Treating The Market as a deity makes it stand outside of human agency and, thus, offers the illusion of its ontological completeness and the futility in attempting its transformation. Missing here is that as a human system, The Market requires human agency for its creation and maintenance. What human beings bring into being we can also take out of being.

Recall the example of disciplinary decadence. Where the discipline is ontologized, there is nothing its practitioners can do but work within it. Where it is understood as a human system, as a living expression of human actions, it could then be transformed through its practitioners' willingness to go beyond it. As we have seen, I call this a "teleological suspension of disciplinarity." It means going beyond a discipline for the sake of purposes that transcend it. Where disciplines are created to address human relationships with reality, such a purposeful suspension of the discipline could be for the sake of furthering our relationship with reality. Returning to market reductionism, the question of suspending notions of market completeness means placing accountability onto agents of The Market, which would transform The Market into a specific kind of prefered market. Deontologized, other considerations can be explored and communicated, which makes capitalism particularized and brought under account as a human-produced system.

Given these criticisms of fetishized capitalism, the reader may wonder about fetishized socialism.[3] The argument thus far is that it is a fallacy when it comes to human institutions, ranging from disciplines to economies, to presume there is one size that fits all. For socialism to work, one must be willing to interrogate what "work" means and confront the possibility that what that means may have conditions under which it fails.[4] This is because, at least as an economic system, it represents a specific form of market among others since even in socialism and, for that matter, communism, there must be some form of exchange. Without such, each individual would have to be self-sufficient and, eventually, isolated as a god onto her, his, or itself. This would contradict the communicability and community premise of communism and the social one of socialism.

We arrive, then, at a problem of at least the western side of the Euromodern world. The rise of capitalism brought along its forms of subjectivity. This includes its philosophical anthropology, which for the most part is the individual consuming subject. This subject brought along with it a position toward political life. As premised on legitimacy through and onto itself, such an individualized subject cannot articulate objectivity and reality because that would require being accountable to something beyond itself. If it makes itself objective and all that is real, the concepts would collapse. There would be no subjectivity from which objectivity could make sense and vice versa. The same would happen to the real and the nonreal. Thus, if conceding there is a world of others, what that subject must do is question the hold they may have on the individual self through creating a form of nominalism of the world. In other words, there are physical things of which some are *selves onto themselves* and, beyond that, a world of differing ways of relating to them. It is not long before truth is jeopardized and what at best could be offered in the company of others is "opinion."[5] This is a mark of the Anglo-philosophical tradition for which Thomas Hobbes is the father and John Stuart Mill one of its finest sons; its connection to capitalism and the position toward political life it engendered is evident in Euromodern liberal political theory, which grew out of this philosophical anthropology. As politics, classically under-stood, involved power as manifested in speech and negotiated conflicts and social aims for flourishing depending on such practices of communication, the threat of conflict via dissent made politics also a threat to what self-sustaining models of the individual sought—namely, the individual's own security and appetite. The consumer-individual increasingly prevailed, and as accountability pointed back to that individual, the decline of collective responsibility meant more direct normative models of morality and force of law supervened. In short, liberal political theory, as we saw in our discussion of John Rawls's thought, is an effort to make morality and law supervene over politics.

This supervenience created an important split, the consequences of which are suffered into the present. The clear statement of this division was in the 18th-century French parliament, where Monarchists sat on the right and republicanists on the left. This right and left separation, although at first arbitrary, had psychoanalytical significance, since "right" also refers to being straight in a society where "left" suffered from superstitions and taboo. In French, the words were *droit* and *gauche*. *Gauche* had replaced the earlier *senestre,* which, as it sounds, was from the Latin *sinister* (literally, to the left). *Droit* has origins in the Latin *directus* ("straight"), which is the past participle of *dirigere* ("to set straight"). We see in this etymological exercise a portrait of two fundamentally different responses to crises. A crisis, after all, refers to a situation in which a decision must be made. Some people's response is to attempt to set things straight. This presumes that which is not straight is a deviation from an initial straight or right position. Setting things straight, therefore, has an implicit "again" in it and, thus, a return. There is, there-fore, an inherent conservative turn in moving to the right, and that involves the associations of rightness such as law and order. The term *droit*, after all, also refers to legal rightness. The right, then, is about a form of rectitude of law and order embedded in an imagined right past. Although conservatives tend to seek order through returning to traditional values, another group—neoconservatives—demands more and, thus, becomes right of traditional conservatives.[6] Since order supervenes, this means threats to it—such as dis-sent, freedom, liberty—must be subordinated. If radicalized, this means all oppositions, all difference, all dissent, all things rendered external threats, must be eliminated. The result is fascism.[7]

There is also an interpretation of keeping straight instead of resetting as straight. This model, which John Rawls called being "well-ordered," is a core one of liberal thought. It is also simultaneously a conservative one in that to maintain straightness requires conserving or preserving it. Thus, the rightward turn of resetting things straight would be interpreted here as transforming what is already straight. The conflict, then, becomes one of how the moment of crisis is interpreted.

This leaves the leftward turn. The left look at liberalism and positions moving right of it as wrong responses to each of their moments. The past and the present, from this perspective, are both imperfect and, thus, required and still require work. In fact, there is no perfect moment but instead those of perfecting or at least making moments better. The left, thus, at first agree with Freud's observation that "Conservatism, however, is too often a welcome excuse of lazy minds, loath to adapt to fast-changing conditions."[8] Leftward thought is future-oriented with the understanding of each future moment being different than the present. Where the goal is to make things better, it is progressive. Where being progressive is interpreted as leading to an imagined perfection—a utopia—there is paradoxically the return of conservatism, for what else is there to do with perfection but to maintain it?

The leftward position also raises questions of liberty and freedom. This is because for change to be possible, there must be something that people could do that diverges from what people have done. There must be possibility or possibilities with the ability to make the new come into being. This ability to bring in the new requires liberty and the possibility of freedom. It has liberty because it must unlock the grips of the past and the present. Where it remains negative in the sense of unlocking or perhaps destroying, its goal becomes an absence of constraints. Radicalized, this model of leftism promises anarchy. Going through the complicated varieties of anarchy averred over the past few hundred years would take us too far afield.[9] For now, the crucial consideration is that where anarchy emerges and each individual is not a god, the only recourse is for some kind of voluntary collective management of life resources. It is not long before one realizes that what is voluntary can be dissolved without compulsory—that is, forced—maintenance. This is where conservatism and libertarianism meet, and where both could also meet fascism. After all, fascism is a voluntary, though also often pressured, association of fascists. This portrait requires, then, a leftward turn in which liberty alone is not the goal. It requires an understanding of freedom that is richer than an absence of constraints.

Imagine the plight of prisoners. When released, they have liberty. When they escape, they also have liberty. The first have more liberty because the second must avoid being seen by those seeking to capture and reincarcerate them. Whether paroled or an escapee, both also often seek the same thing—to go home. This "place" or set of relationships of belonging is where people could live and at times flourish. It requires the empowering of possibility. There are people who have traumatic associations with their place of belonging. One could say they belong to those places in the form of abuse and suffering. The response is that such places are perversions of home. They introduce the paradox of nonbelonging forms of belonging or belonging by virtue of not belonging. The outcome of either is the same—some form of escape. They are, thus, not homes properly understood, except for the masochists who may need degradation as affirmation of the familiar. Rejecting that, the course of belonging through places of flourishing entails possibility, and this, then, leads to concepts such as growth and maturation. The latter is crucial here since maturation involves understanding the false dilemma of dystopia versus utopia. Life is not a case of the depressing versus the ideal. It is the rejected alongside the aspired. It is also one of building what is reasonable in the face of weaknesses and strengths. Seeing both facilitates a dialectical relationship to reality in which there are not always two competing universals of the positive and the negative but instead an interactive relationship of both. What, we should then ask, as we did with capitalism, would be the philosophical anthropology of that leftward turn? It would be no less than, as we have been seeing throughout these reflections, the ongoing realization of incomplete subjectivity, of taking responsibility for a future that is never foreclosed or overdetermined but instead must be built paradoxically through and beyond one's immediate reach.

We come, then, to a fundamental distinction of right and left. The right, after all, decides within a temporal realm of immediate reach. This means for the right it all comes back to the proverbial "me," which is why others are often jeopardized. A similar path emerges for the various sliding locations of liberal identification. The leftward turn is distinguished, as well, by an immediate and a far-reaching temporality. The immediate one tends to grasp for what "we"—understood as those in the here and now—can reach and thus eventually back to "me." That is why some forms of left could slide easily into the right. Another kind realizes that a far-reaching temporality offers a place into which one cannot enter yet could only come about from the actions of immediate and succeeding generations. The relationship of subjects, thus, becomes a place between the known and the anonymous. In this second model is a clue to political responsibility and political action. As it is always about us and those who are not us, the ramifications of such actions are responsibilities for those who are always eventually unknown. Without a forecasted outcome of who they are and what they would receive, action becomes an existential challenge. It requires commitment without foreknowledge of outcome. It is political action that is, in the language of Kierkegaard, a leap of faith.

A leap of faith requires infinite resignation. This means the conviction of no guarantee of anything on the other side to catch us. No epistemic or moral mediation. This is why Kierkegaard considered a teleological suspension of the ethical. It does not mean that ethical life disappears. It simply means it lacks justifications or mediations through which it gains its legitimacy and that taking the leap requires taking full responsibility for that leap. This is an ancient insight. It is there in Judaism. It is there in Buddhist, Hindu, and Islamic thought. It is there all across the world because human beings have always been haunted by a displeasing truth. We do not only face responsibility in the world but also our responsibility for that responsibility. In other words, that responsibility was ultimately not handed to or demanded of us despite many comforting mythologies, prophesies, and rationalizations we have developed to convince us of such. A teleological suspension of disciplinarity and the idols of our age initiates responsibility, even at metalevels, for the justifications of justification. At political levels, this means there is no mediating force of promised political outcomes to grasp. It means the commitment itself is the responsibility through which responsibility for responsibility is made manifest.

This is scary stuff. As Ali Shariati observed: "This act is neither logical nor illogical, it is alogical...."[10] Some recoil from such a possibility and thus reject political responsibility and the political subject—we who are all politically responsible—for the immediate security of individual responsibility in the forms of legal and morally responsible ones.[11] The political is, for them, too open. They want the closed security of rule. At most, instead of the political, they prefer well-regulated spheres in which politics may occur. This expectation of rule over the political is the proffered model of liberal, conservative, neoconservative, and, where politics is minimized as much as possible to the point of being eliminated, fascist thought. Among liberals, the proffered philosophical anthropology becomes a moral, and often moralized, one of moral individual subjects. Neoliberalism, building upon this view, strives for a combination of The Market and civil liberties focusing on individual moral subjects with individual rights. The conservative wants that subject to be constrained by tradition, the neoconservative by law and order, and the fascist demands no deviation from its total and ultimately tyrannical dictates.

As the liberal subject is already shown to be an extension of The Market subject, we could imagine what follows. First, the idea of morality prevailing becomes the model of avowed normative political theory. This ultimately means eliminating the contingency of politics and, consequently, politics itself. Second, where politics is claimed but ultimately rejected, the task becomes its transformation under market constraints. This requires constructing a marketable political subject. Where that occurs, the most compatible kind is the moral one posing as political. The political seems to reappear here except that it is devoid of the contingency that animates it. Where to be political is to be moral, the logic of moral subjectivity, often as a constrained or regulated one, emerges.

Unfortunately, as we have seen, moral subjects often become moralistic ones through an expectation of moral purity. This offers notions of innocence, and the result is a world in which one could either be free of having done harm or be those who are harmed.[12] The victimized subject as the moral subject follows, and appearance—at least in the avowed political realm—becomes premised on having been harmed. The logic here is legalistic in form, and in fact that is what emerges: politics as a case of petitioned redress for harm. This destroys the political dimensions of political life, since, after all, the key subject of political life is the citizen, the agent of citizenship, the person whose appearance depends on actions on which the life of power depends. The citizen, qua citizen, need not be a victim. The citizen must foremost be capable. Thus, the moralistic model is ultimately at war with citizenship and politics, but it is ironic here since it is offered as political in a world of commodified politics. One's political marketability becomes one's victimization or harm. This is why, as we see in today's ultimately postmodern reassertion of fascism, white hegemonic groups claim to be victims.[13] It is why, in fact, there are so many victims or harmed subjects everywhere. We live in an age of global victimization. It is not that there are not actually people who are harmed and victimized. It is that their harm and victimization are being weaponized at the expense of political life. As even birth is traumatic, one wonders who ultimately escapes harm in any meaningful sense. It announces a claim on the basis of what one is (among the harmed) instead of what one can do (citizenship or political work). It also leads to a cruel response to actual suffering, such as what is being experienced in detention and refugee camps, in the plight of the many disposed and damned of the earth: ignoring them. *Their* suffering, through being rendered illegitimate—because of them being rendered illicit people—becomes invisible. Despite all the moralism, empathy is in short supply.

This development of the subordination of politics through the supervenience of moralistic subjectivity is an expression of political nihilism. It is symptomatic of present-day social decadence.

Shifting the Geography of Reason, Shifting the Geography of Action

A conclusion thus far in this analysis of decadence and its teleological suspension is that the degradation of political life holds within it forces of disempowerment. This means that although a triumphant moralism surfaces—as we have seen historically with assertions of human rights as a feature of why liberal governing and economic models should be preserved—there is a paradoxical undermining of democracy in many liberal democracies in the name of democracy. What, after all, is the point of an avowed moral democracy when it offers no power to the people? Of course, much depends on what "people" means here, since moral subjects could also be people. I write "could also be" because, as attested to in capitalist societies, corporations are legally persons and often have more rights, especially as witnessed in the United States during the COVID-19 pandemic of 2020, than people of flesh and blood. What is significant is that political subjects as people are on the decline. How do we know? A significant sign of disempowerment is where agents then focus on their agency. Where political life is healthy, their energy moves outward and interacts with the ever-widening reach of the social world, its institutions, and its communicability. Where political life is jeopardized, the movement is inward. Eventually, agency is a manifestation of the ability to act on the self, and where even that is jeopardized, it becomes the body devoid of selfhood.

The language of "bodies" is one striking feature of contemporary discourse, especially, unfortunately, among the racialized left, although its influence crosses many demographics. Its impact is global. Everywhere, there are people trying to fix themselves, as their ability to transform the societies and institutions that affect them evaporates. This development is connected to the observations on the right and the left. The right is willing to sacrifice liberties—even lives—for the sake of an avowed secure world of law and order. This means being willing to use coercive mechanisms, ranging from batons, tanks, and teargas, to petitioning the use of "heat rays," to destroy sources of dissidence.[14] It means also a war on freedom and its institutional manifestation—namely, political life. It requires governing and rule over politics. Since Euromodern conservatism and turns to the right endorse capitalism, this path also takes the form of global privatization. Its historical reasons are manifold.

Thinking back to the 1960s into mid-1970s, the idea of a globally free and humane world was part of the Zeitgeist. Proponents of capitalism were not pleased. They knew such developments would require global democratic structures in which there would be nowhere for capital to turn for the extraction of profits from alienated labor. Large federal structures could ally with each other to form even larger ones through which ultimately there would be a mere agreement to create planetary political life. Everything from environmental regulation to universal health care would be a possibility. Even in a globally mixed economy such as democratic socialism, the eventual task of keeping labor for the production of wealth would emerge, and that would mean the subordination of capital to the lives of people and other forms of life on the planet. The response was to hijack crucial concepts through which global democracy could be understood. One of those was the notion of the "global." The success of the think tanks, corporate investments, and organized coups for this cause is evident in today's equivocation of the word "global" with privatization.[15]

Accompanying this triumph is a host of hijacked concepts. The reader may notice my use of the word "Euromodern" throughout. Recall that this is because, as we have seen, the word "modern" has been coopted to mean "European" or "Western," when all the term once meant was "present." To be present meant to be centrally linked to the time to come. Not to be so was to be past. Euromodern colonization and enslavement of much of the planet led to the presupposition of humanity's future being a European or Western one, and thus the presumption was that the modern and European/Western were the same. Yet, before there was a geopolitical idea of

Europe or Western, there were many countries in which their people understood themselves as belonging to the present and having a future. When other countries imposed themselves upon others, the question of whether the dominated countries would remain, disappear, or some mixed form would succeed arose. In the case of Indigenous peoples, where conquest was the model, the future imposed upon them was that of the settlers. This rendered Indigenous peoples as belonging to the past and pejorative notions of primitivism prevailed. Where the Indigenous peoples saw their situation as one of invasion, the idea of continued struggle for the future transformed their present. There would then be no primitives but instead the question of which kind of future-formed life to live. This future may even transcend the Indigenous/settler nonrelationship. It is a nonrelationship because it is premised on reciprocal universals that do not meet; it is a Manichean separation of complete positivity and absolute negativity. Interaction explodes this binary and the question of relationships means no one's remaining the same.

The hijacking of the global led to a form of leftwing allergy to the global and power. This is because the global is often equated with privatization, and power became the coercive mechanisms of its implementation. The opposite became "local" and antipower. This was (and continues to be) a mistake. This is because it closed off the imaginative possibility of a global public, with public institutions of global flourishing. It also reduced power to the rightwing model of coercion. As that model is the acquisition of power through the disempowering of others, one should ask what would eliminating disempowerment entail. What would that be other than empowering the once disempowered? This means imaginative and political work should be about extending the potential of flourishing forms of power. It is, in other words, a teleological suspension of power, where decadent power (coercive power) is transcended for the sake of open power (empowering freedom).

This global reflection raises geopolitical dimensions of power, and since thought and deed must meet in such a quest, it also raises the question of the geography of reason. That reason, where subjugated for the purposes of coercive power, calls for transformation and the location of agents through which it could be manifested. It requires a move from self-contained hording models to relational ones of building open relations. It demands, as we have seen, shifting the geography of reason.

To understand shifting the geography of reason we must first consider what "geography of reason" is. Drawing upon Enrique Dussel's concept of "the underside of modernity"—where colonized peoples stand as those unseen "below," there is a dialectical aspect of living in or being located at the underside of any condition or epoch.[16] If we look at history, among those from the underside usually are those with ideas that hold the key to the future. Those on the surface imagine themselves to be where humanity is going, as we saw with the confusion of Euromodernity with modernity. When they fall, they often watch their world serving as the outline for another to come, and it is often one with which they do not identify. Yet, we should notice, each empire left its unique traces that were historically transformed. There were Roman roads and aqueducts. There were the Arab and Chinese trade routes. Across ancient Africa there were trade routes from Kmt, Nubia, and Axum, through to the past millennium in Songhai, Mali, and others across the central coast. And more recently, there were the ocean routes of the Portuguese and Spaniards from which the Danes, Dutch, and British built theirs. Those countries, born in the transformation of Christendom into Europe, forced themselves onto the outlines of those in Abya Yala, and others grew out of their colonies. The United States and former Soviet Union sprung from the outlines of Britain to the west and the conflicts from the various imperial forces of Europe and their allies in the east. Beyond nation-states and formal imperial geopolitical units, why could not it also be the case that shifts from sailing ships to steam engines, from coal to oil and gasoline to electricity, silicone, and information technologies not have their own outlines—as products of various imperial efforts—through which creative people from the South could articulate different futures?

Part of the arrogance of all empires is that they imagine they could open doors that lead one-way. The architects of the global advancement of privatized capital imagined using information technology such as the Internet for unilateral flows of capital. Doors and keys are, however, technologies with possibilities beyond those initially posed. They combined with various pathways and offered contexts through which imagination and deed could build a different and perhaps better kind of tomorrow. Unexpected paths could facilitate discoveries along the way.

Taking hold of building alternative futures requires a commitment to having a future at all. Where the geography of reason means that only certain groups of people, in a specific geopolitical location called "the North," have a future and reason, the structure of the relationship is reason's supposedly coming "down" to the people of "the South." The implications are many. One is the presumption that people from the North offer through reason the ideas—concepts, knowledge, theory—that make people of the South socially and politically appear. Those from the South thus become passive recipients of such intellectual light. This is a distortion of history and reality. It erases facts, and it cultivates dependency. It also leads, since the people of the North avowedly use reason to illuminate their experience, to the conclusion that Northern experience is more epistemologically valuable than Southern ones. If the point is to bring reason to experience, then everyone must take responsibility for reason and the theory it creates. It is this taking responsibility for reason that leads to the shift. It is crucially done without permission of those who attempt to horde reason. But here is the additional shift. The horded reason is a distorted reason. It is a form of unreasonable reason that imagines itself complete and standing on its own. Those who challenge it do so from an understanding of reason as an ongoing relationship and commitment to certain kinds of practices that are, thus, unlike this distorted reason, never "complete." In such a challenge, even the future is open. They thus, in shifting the location/geography of reason, also shift reason itself from a closed to an open, relational project.

The implications of these shifts are many. They involve challenging even notions of "location." There are Southern elements in the geographical North—as we see in Eastern Europe and also the many migrant and refugee groups across the world—and there are Northern ones in the South, as we see with settlers in the South and the disasters and coups and antidemocratic directions of privatization elites coopting countries such as Brazil and India. All of these are marked by historical inheritance from colonialism, enslavement, and racism.[17]

Another shift is, as we have seen, the notion of "modern." The portrait I gave reveals that to be modern—present—one must transform or shift one's understanding of belonging. One must belong to the future, which offers meaning to one's present and one's past. This means, then, that if Europe and its North American and Australian exemplars are not *the future* but instead only a part of it, then the modern that has dominated the world for the past few centuries is simply the Euromodern and understanding this is already a shift in the geography of reason. Indeed, it enables us, as we have seen, to look at past moderns and modernities. If we were to use a time machine and go to the Mediterranean of antiquity and consult their maps, we would need to turn many of them upside down to recognize the regions and countries. Those maps reveal that people used to look "up" to the southern hemisphere. Africa was "above" what we now call Europe. We could imagine how various peoples in the southern hemisphere, such as Australasia, thought of "up" geographically. Our world, then, is a transformation of one form of what was once modern for another, and we would be deluding ourselves if we were to think of the Euromodern as the last word on this process.

So, finally, if we think about reason as an incomplete but ongoing project, we could see why *shifting*, instead of simply a shift, in the geography of reason is a contemporary task of social and historical transformation. This shifting is a living, ongoing project premised on a commitment to building livable worlds of living thought.

Shifting the geography of reason also requires thinking anew and creatively how we understand concepts such as "right" and "left." Recall there are left-wing positions that can slide to the right when we understand their goals. Conservatism, we have seen, is a turn toward a past, a cherry-picked past, of supposed security, law, order, and perfection. This often requires eliminating sources of dissent such as difference, creativity, and freedom and, if pushed to its extreme, cultivating fascism. We should understand that the world of the 21st century is not like those of the past. Too many people respond to these crises through trying to figure out which past century to which they belong—the 20th, 19th, or 18th. Our world, we should bear in mind, is undergoing its own seismic shifts; with nearly eight billion people and technologies that traverse distances in a nano-second, we live on a smaller planet. We are compressing reality and, thus, risk imploding life.

Among the questions we face is the challenge of living on a planet incapable of sustaining the kind of life to which past ages have committed us—and to which those who wish to return by turning to the right are condemning us—to, as Sri Aurobindo put it, opening up our minds to our potential to address our challenges.[18] The late political theorist Benjamin Barber summarized the situation thus: "Nature doesn't negotiate."[19] We must understand that the challenges we face today are human produced; they are manifestations of power by which human beings could affect life beyond ourselves. That means they require human action for their transformation, and the human world of produced power is, as we have seen, properly called politics. The right's effort to eliminate political life imperils us all—and so, too, certain forms of revolutionary left fantasies of concluding the path of history, a project that ultimately slides back into the right—but, as I have been arguing, we cannot address such a challenge through leaving the understanding of power, as has occurred with "global," in their hands. They assert power as exclusively coercive. It would be a mistake for the rest of us to adopt such a view. Coercive power disempowers. To fight against disempowerment requires empowerment. Shifting the geography of reason requires understanding that power should not be reduced to a single element but instead should be explored to its creative potential. If we acknowledge power as the ability to make things happen and securing access to the conditions of doing so, there is much proverbially to be done.

We should remember that if we think of the work to be done simply as that of elimination, of reaction, to the right, our course could lead to a form of anarchy in which we become small, privatized protectorates—in short, again, a left that becomes the right. We need a responsible form of practice attuned to the many dimensions of what we are and our relationship to other forms of life. We need to unleash our capacity to create, to build meaning, while being sober to the realities of the terrestrial creatures we are. This requires not only a shift in the geography of reason but also an understanding of the fragility of life in its wider context.

What might that be? Think of us as specks of dust on a speck of dust in a cloud of dust in a larger constellation of dust in a vast universe or possible pluriverse through which our future depends on our understanding that our little speck of dust is our world reaching out for others and that we are also dependent, in the end, on each other.

A Concluding Consideration

We come, then, to a repeated theme throughout this reflection. Shifting the geography reason demands a shift in our understanding of responsibility. Much of our planet is locked in the language of legal and moral responsibility inherited from the rise of Euromodern colonialism and its competing organizing systems locked in reductive models of nature along with metaphysical idols. We need to understand the uniqueness of political responsibility, which, as the late Iris Marion Young stressed, is always about the future.[20] Since I have argued that political life always raises the question of those who are anonymous—the not yet born or arrived and many among those who have become ancestors—we should understand what it means to fight for what is not about us individually but instead about what depends on us while transcending us. We often forget what haunts human hubris. Each of us is a descendant of those who not only stood upright and developed tools and language but also realized the importance of nonnarcissistic love. Narcissistic love seeks mirrors. Political love offers no such flattery, self-indulgence, and gratification. The future is never *ours*. It is a love always committed to the life and freedom of others.

Notes

1. See, for example, Lorraine Boissoneault, "Colored Pigments and Complex Tools Suggest Humans Were Trading 100,000 Years Earlier Than Previously Believed," *Smithsonian Magazine* (15 March 2018): https://www.smithsonian-mag.com/science-nature/colored-pigments-and-complex-tools-suggest-human-trade-100000-years-earlier-previously-believed-180968499/; Matt Ridley, *The Rational Optimist: How Prosperity Evolves*, Reprint Edition (London, UK: Harper Perennial, 2011); Yval Noah Harari, *Sapiens: A Brief History of Humankind* (London, UK: Harper Perennial, 2018). And, of course, the classic overview of the history of theoretical economics, Robert L. Heilbroner's classic, *The Worldly Philosophers: The Lives, Times, and Ideas of the Great Economic*, Revised 7th Edition (New York, NY: Simon & Schuster, 1999 [original 1953]), see Ellen Meiksins Woods's *Democracy Against Capitalism: Renewing Historical Materialism* (London, UK: Verso, 2016) and *The Origin of Capitalism: A Longer View* (London, UK: Verso, 2017) and Paul Bowles, *Capitalism* (Edinburgh Gate, UK: Pearson Longman, 2007) for discussions addressing themes such as globalization and regional kinds of capitalism in post-socialist societies.

2. See, for example, Lewis R. Gordon, "The Market Colonization of Intellectuals," *truthout* (Tuesday, 6 April 2010): http://archive.truthout.org/the-market-colonization-intellectuals58310. This is also an insight of James Boggs in his *American Revolution: Pages from a Negro Worker's Notebook*, 2nd Edition (New York, NY: Monthly Review Press, 2009 [1963]).

3. Herbert Marcuse famously offered a critique of capitalism *and* socialism in his analysis of the social effects of hyper-industrialization in *One-Dimensional Man: Studies in the Ideology of Advanced Industrial Society* (Boston, MA: Beacon Press, 1964).

4. For elaboration of this issue, see, for example, Madina Tlostanova, *What Does It Mean to Be Post-Soviet?: Decolonial Art from the Ruins of the Soviet Empire* (Durham, NC: Duke University Press, 2018) and Rastko Močnik, "Beyond Fascism?: Historical Parallels and Structural Specificities of Post-Socialism," *Tiempo devorado: revista de historia actual* 4, no. 1 (2017): 146–165, which explore the Eastern European context. James Boggs's *American Revolution: Pages from a Negro Worker's Notebook*, 2nd Edition (New York, NY: Monthly Review Press, 2009 [1963]), explores this question in the North American context.

5. Among the classic discussions of this phenomenon is José Ortega y Gasset's *The Revolt of the Masses* (New York, NY: W.W. Norton, 1994 [1929]). For discussion of its more recent manifestation, see Michael P. Lynch, *Know-It-All Society: Truth and Arrogance in Political Culture* (New York, NY: W.W. Norton, 2019).

6. Jack Kerwick, *Misguided Guardians: The Conservative Case against Neoconservatism* (Las Vegas, NV: Stairway Press, 2016).

7. Elaboration on fascism and the many debates over its meaning and usefulness as a description of contemporary right-wing extremism and "populism" would take us too far afield here. For discussions of these debates, see Vladimir Milisavljević and Natalija Mićunović (eds.), *Xenophobia, Identity and New Forms of Nationalism* (Belgrade, Serbia: Institute of Social Science, 2019) and Jason Stanley, *How Fascism Works* (New York, NY: Random House, 2018). There is also illumination through its opposition, anti-fascism, as offered in Bill V. Mullen and Christopher Vials (eds.), *The U.S. Anti-fascism Reader* (London, UK: Verso, 2020).

8. Sigmund Freud, *Dream Psychology: Psychoanalysis for Beginners*, trans. Montague David Eder (New York, NY: James McCann, 2013), iii.

9. For an overview, see, e.g., Peter Marshall, *Demanding the Impossible: A History of Anarchism* (Oakland, CA: PM Press, 2010). One would hope that studies of anarchy would not fall into the pitfalls of epistemic conservatism with regard to the intellectual history of the subject offered by people of color, but, sadly, that would be naïve. Primary source supplements would include, for example, Lucy Parsons, *Lucy Parsons: Freedom, Equality & Solidarity—Writings & Speeches, 1878–1937*, Gale Aherns and Roxanne Dunbar-Ortiz (eds.) (Chicago, IL: Charles H. Kerr Publishing, 2004) and the writings He-Yin Zhen, some of which are available in English in Lydia H. Liu, Rebecca E. Karl, and Dorthy Ko (eds.), *The Birth of Chinese Feminism: Essential Texts in Transnational Theory* (New York, NY: Columbia University Press, 2013), 53–186.

10. Ali Shariati, *Man and Islam*, trans. Fatolla Marjani (North Haedon, NJ: Islamic Publication International, 1981), 61.

11. Karl Jaspers, *Die Schuldfrage,* available in English as *The Question of German Guilt*, trans. E.B. Ashton (New York, NY: Fordham University Press, 2000 [1947]) *and* Iris Marion Young, "Responsibility and Global Labor Justice," *The Journal of Political Philosophy* 12, no. 4 (2004): 365–388.

12. Appeals to national innocence also offers notions of collective exceptionalism, of which American innocence is a prime example, as Ipek S. Burnett argues in *A Jungian Inquiry into the American Psyche: The violence of Innocence* (New York, NY: Routledge, 2019).

13. The examples are too many, of which undergirding recent developments is the rise of fascism under the guise of populism and alt-right from Brazil to the United Kingdom to the United States. Think of the absurdity and hysteria behind white supremacist claims of "white genocide" that accompany some of these moments. For discussion, see Rosa Schwartzburg, "No, There Isn't a White Genocide," *Jacobin* (4 September 2019): https://www.jacobinmag.com/2019/09/white-genocide-great-replacement-theory and James Pogue, "The Myth of White Genocide," *Harper's Magazine* (15 February 2019), posted in *The Pulitzer Center*: https://pulitzercenter.org/reporting/myth-white-genocide.

14. See Tim Elfrink, "Safety and Ethics Worries Sidelined a 'Heat Ray' for Years. The Feds Asked about Using It on Protesters," *The Washington Post* (17 September 2020): https://www.washingtonpost.com/nation/2020/09/17/heat-ray-protesters-trump-dc/

15. For a study, see Enrique Prieto Rios, "Thinking on International Investment Law: From Colonialism to International Systemic Violence" (Doctoral Dissertation, Birkbeck, University of London, 2017).

16. Enrique Dussel, *The Underside of Modernity: Apel, Ricoeur, Rorty, Taylor, and the Philosophy of Liberation*, trans Eduardo Mendieta (Atlantic Highlands, NJ: Humanities International Press, 1996).
17. For elaboration, see Jane Anna Gordon, *Statelessness and Contemporary Enslavement* (New York, NY: Routledge, 2020).
18. Sri Aurobindo, *The Future Evolution of Man: The Divine Life Upon Earth* (Twin Lakes, WI: Lotus Press, 1963).
19. Benjamin Barber, *Cool Cities* (New Haven, CT: Yale University Press, 2017), 6.
20. Iris Marion Young, "Responsibility and Global Labor Justice."

Chapter 5

Thoughts on Afropessimism

Afropessimism grew into an influential area of black thought by the second decade of the new millennium. The term "Afropessimism," as I am using it here, came out of "Afro-pessimism." The elimination of the hyphen is an important development since it dispels ambiguity and in effect announces a specific mode of thought. Should the hyphen remain, the ambiguity would be between pessimistic people of African descent and philosophical or theoretical pessimism.[1] The conjoined, theoretical term is what proponents of that intellectual movement often have in mind in their diagnosis of what I shall call "the black condition."

The appeal to a black condition is peculiarly existential, though it is done in this context in ironic ways. Existentialists, after all, as is well known, reject notions of human "nature," on the grounds that human beings live in a world of possibility, which makes an essentialist notion such as "nature" a matter, at least for such realities, always in the making.[2] In the classic formulation, human reality exists *prior* to its essence. For each human being, essence is, as it were, an appointment whose actuality is not always fulfilled. Such a task does not mean that human beings lack anchorage. Everyone has to start from somewhere and that or those are conditions of possibility for a human world. Existentialists, thus, often prefer to speak or write of "human condition" or *conditions* for these reasons. What human beings produce is manifold, but key in every instance is a mode of life, a world, so to speak, in and through which human beings could emerge as human. Human beings thus, for the most part, produce human realities and worlds (whether good or bad). Such realities and worlds offer a network of relations and relationships through which many other things are produced, all of which are constellations of meaning. Again, what comes about could be appreciated or rejected, but either is valuable or not in terms of how meaningful it is for ongoing human projects. There is, thus, also a very pragmatic dimension to this existential portrait of what is also called "human reality."

Critics of existentialism often reject its *human* formulation. Heidegger, for instance, in his "Letter on Humanism," lambasted Sartre for supposedly in effect subordinating Being to a philosophical anthropology with dangers of anthropocentrism.[3] Yet, as I have argued in a variety of writings, a philosophical understanding of culture raises the problem of the conditions through which philosophical reflections become meaningful.[4] Though a human activity, a more radical understanding of culture raises the question of the human being as the producer of an open reality. If the human being is in the making, then "human reality" is never complete and is more the relations in which such thought takes place than a claim about the thought. Additionally, what Heidegger fails to understand is, as Keiji Nishitani reminds us, Being is not all it is cracked up to be, as it also covers over instead of reveal reality.[5] That includes human reality.

The etymology of *existence* already points to these elements. From the Latin *ex sistere*, "to stand out," it also means to appear; against invisibility in the stream of effects through which the human world appears, much follows through the creative and at times alchemic force of human thought and deed.

Quarrels with and against existential thought are many. In more recent times, they have surfaced primarily from Marxists, structuralists, and poststructuralists, even though there were, and continue to be, many existential Marxists and even existentialists with structuralist and poststructuralist leanings and tendencies.[6]

I begin with this tale of philosophical abstraction to contextualize, at least in philosophical terms, Afropessimism. Its main exemplars, such as Jared Sexton and Frank Wilderson III, began their careers with training in academic literary theory, an area dominated by poststructualism since the 1970s through recent times in the Northern academies, even in many cases that avow "Marxism." Sexton and Wilderson divert from a reductive poststructuralism, or at least attempt to do so, through examining important existential moves inaugurated, as Daniel McNeil observed, by Frantz Fanon and his intellectual heirs.[7]

The critical question that Afropessimism addresses in this fusion is the viability of posed strategies of Black liberation. (I am using the capital "B" here to point not only to the racial designation "black" but also to the emancipatory one "Black." Afropessimists often mean both, since blacks and Blacks have a central and centered role in their thought.) The world that produced blacks and in consequence Blacks is, for Afropessimists, a crushing historical one whose Manichaean divide is sustained contraries best kept segregated. There is not only epistemic apartheid, as Reiland Rabaka would formulate it, but also ontological apartheid.[8] Worse, any effort of mediation leads, in their view, to confirmed Black subordination and, worse, erasure. Overcoming this requires purging the world of antiblackness, although achieving such would be futile where the black remains since, for them, the black would by definition not "be" there, or, for that matter, *anywhere*.[9]

Where cleansing the world is unachievable, an alternative is to disarm the force of antiblack racism. Where whites lack power over Blacks, they lose relevance—at least politically and at levels of cultural and racial capital or hegemony. This is a position I have argued since my first book *Bad Faith and Antiblack Racism.*[10] Wilderson joins me in that critique through exploring my concept of "an antiblack world" to build similar arguments. Sexton makes similar moves, although with a focus on the thought of the sociologist Orlando Patterson, in his discussions of "social death."[11] The rest of this chapter is an exploration of some nonexhaustive criticisms I have of the Afropessimist versions of these arguments, which may be of some use for readers interested in this area of thought.

The first is that *"an* antiblack world" is not identical with *"the world is antiblack."* The latter is an antiblack racist *project.* It is not the historical *achievement* of such. Its limitations emerge from a basic fact. Black people and other opponents of such an enterprise fought, and continue to fight, against it. The same argument applies to the argument about social death. Such an achievement would have rendered even those authors' and the reflections I am offering here stillborn. The basic premises of the antiblack world and social death arguments are, then, locked in performative contradictions. They fail at the moment they are *articulated.* Yet, they have rhetorical force. This is evident through the continued growth of its proponents, literature, and forums devoted to it, in which all lay claim to stillborn status.

In *Bad Faith and Antiblack Racism,* I argued that there are forms of antiblack racism that are also offered under the guise of love. I was writing about whites who exoticize blacks while offering themselves as white sources of black salvation. It was a response to those who regard racism exclusively as acts of demonization. There are also racist forms of valorization. Analyzed in terms of bad faith, where one lies to oneself in an attempt to flee displeasing truths for pleasing falsehoods, exoticists romanticize blacks while affirming white normativity and themselves as principals of reality. These ironic, performative contradictions are features of all forms of racism, where one group is elevated to a godlike status and another is pushed below or outside that of human despite both claiming to be human.

Antiblack racism offers whites self–other relations (necessary for ethics) with each other but not so for groups forced in a "zone of nonbeing" below or outside them. Although to be outside is not necessarily to be below, it is so in a system of hierarchy in which above is also interpreted as being within. There is asymmetry where whites and any designated racially superior groups stand as others who look downward to those who are not *their* others or their analogs. Antiblack racism is, thus, not a problem of blacks being "others." It is a problem of their *not-being-analogical-selves-and-not-even-being-others.*

Fanon, in *Black Skin, White Masks,* reminds us that Blacks among each other live in a world of selves and others. It is in attempted relations with whites *under circumstances where whites control the conditions* that these problems of dehumanization and subordination occur. Reason in such contexts, as he observes, has a bad habit of walking out when Blacks enter. What are Blacks to do? As reason cannot be *forced* to recognize Blacks because that would be "violence," they must ironically reason *reasonably* with such forms of unreasonable reason. Contradictions loom. Racism is, given these arguments, a project of imposing nonrelations as the model of dealing with people designated "black."[12]

In *The Damned of the Earth*, Fanon goes further and argues that colonialism is an attempt to impose a Manichean structure of contraries instead of a dialectical one of ongoing, human negotiations of contradictions. The former segregates the groups; the latter is produced from interaction. The police, he observes, is the primary mediator between the two models, as their role is the use of force/violence to maintain the contraries instead of the human, discursive one of politics and civility requiring the elimination of separation through the interactive, and ultimately intimate, dynamics of communication. Such societies draw legitimacy from Black nonexistence or invisibility. Black appearance, in other words, would be a violation of those systems. Think of the continued blight of police, extra-judicial killings of blacks and Blacks in those countries.[13] The ongoing model of fascist white rule as the daily condition of blacks is to prevent the emergence of Blacks.

An immediate observation of many postcolonies is that antiblack attitudes, practices, and institutions are not exclusively white. Black antiblack dispositions make this clear. In addition to black antiblackness taking the form of white hatred of black people, there is also the adoption of black exoticism. Where this exists, blacks simultaneously receive avowed black love alongside black rejection of agency. Many problems follow. The absence of agency bars maturation, which would reinforce the racial logic of blacks as in effect wards of whites. Without agency, ethics, liberation, maturation, politics, and responsibility could not be possible. This is because blacks would not actually be able *to do* anything outside of the sphere of white approbation and commands.

Afropessimism endorses the previous set of observations, but this agreement is supported by a hidden premise of white agency versus black and Black incapacity. They make much of Fanon's remark that "the Black has no ontological resistance in the eyes of the white."[14] Fanon's rhetorical flare led many unfortunate souls to misread this remark. As he had already argued that racism is a socially produced phenomenon, his point was that those who produced it take it to be ontological. In other words, such people—in this case whites—do not take seriously that blacks have any ontological resistance to white points of view. Fanon was not arguing that blacks are ontologically beings, or even nonbeings, of that kind. If this were so, he would not have pointed out, in numerous sections of that book, black and Black experiences with each other. The whole point of the chapter in which that remark is made, "The Lived-Experience of the Black," is to explore *blacks' and Blacks' points of view*. This is a patent rejection of an ontological status while pointing to the presumed ontological status of a skewed perspective.

Proponents of Afropessimism might respond that their position on white agency and black incapacity comes from Fanon's famous remark that though whites created *le Nègre*—the French term for, depending on the context, "negro," "nigger," and "black"—it was *les Nègres* who created Négritude.[15] Whites clearly did not create Afropessimism, which Black liberationists should, in agreement, celebrate. We should avoid the fallacy of confusing the source with the outcome. History is not short of bad ideas from good or well-intentioned people. If intrinsically good, each person of African descent would become ethically and epistemologically a switching of the Manichean contraries, which means in effect only changing the players instead of the racist game. We come, then, to the crux of the matter. If the goal of Afropessimism *is Afropessimism*, its achievement would be attitudinal and, in the language of old, stoic—in short, a symptom of antiblack society.

At this point, there are several observations that follow. The first is a diagnosis of the implications of Afropessimism as a symptom. The second pertains to the epistemological implications of Afropessimism. The third is whether a disposition counts as a political act and, if so, is it sufficient for its avowed aims. There are more, but for the sake of brevity, I will simply focus on these.[16]

An ironic dimension of pessimism is that it is the other side of optimism. Oddly enough, both are connected to nihilism, which is, as Nietzsche showed, a decline of values during periods of social decay.[17] It emerges when people no longer want to be responsible for their actions. The same problem surfaces in movements. When one such as the Black Liberation movement is suffering from decay, nihilism is symptomatic. Familiar tropes follow. Optimists expect intervention from beyond. Pessimists declare that relief is not forthcoming. Neither takes responsibility for what is valued. The *valuing* is what leads to the second, epistemic point. The presumption that what is at stake is what can be *known* to determine what can be done *is* the problem. If such knowledge were possible, the debate would be about who is reading the evidence correctly. Such judgment would be *a priori*—that is, prior to events actually occurring. The future, unlike transcendental conditions such as language, signs, and reality, is *ex post facto*; it is yet to come. Facing the future, the question is not what *will be* or *how do we know what will be* but instead the realization that *whatever is done will be that on which the future will depend*. Rejecting optimism and pessimism, there is a supervening alternative, as we have seen throughout the reflections offered throughout this book—namely, political commitment.

The appeal to political commitment is not only in stream with what French existentialists call *l'intellectuel engagé* (the committed intellectual) but also in what reaches back through the history and existential situation of enslaved, racialized ancestors. Many were, in truth, an existential paradox of commitment to action without guarantees. The slave revolts, micro and macro acts of resistance, escapes, and returns to help others do the same, the cultivated instability of plantations and other forms of enslavement, and countless other actions, were waged against a gauntlet of forces designed to eliminate any hope of success. The claim of colonialists and enslavers was that the future belonged to them, not to the enslaved and the indigenous. Such people were, in colonial eyes, incapable of ontological resistance. A result of more than 500 years of "conquest" and 300 years of enslavement was also a (white) rewriting of history in which African and First Nations' agency was, at least at the level of scholarship, practically erased. Yet there was resistance even in that realm, as Africana and First Nation intellectual history and scholarship attest; what, after all, are Africana, Black, and Indigenous Studies? What, after all, are those many sites of intellectual production and activism outside of hegemonic academies? Such actions set the course for different kinds of struggle today.

Such reflections occasion meditations on the concept of failure. Afropessimism, the existential critique suggests, suffers from a failure in their analysis of failure. Consider Fanon's notion of constructive failure, where what does not initially work transforms conditions for something new to emerge. To understand this argument, one must rethink the philosophical anthropology at the heart of a specific line of Euromodern thought on what it means to be human. Atomistic and individual-substance-based, this model, articulated by Thomas Hobbes, John Locke, John Stuart Mill, and many others, is of a nonrelational being that thinks, acts, and moves along a course in which continued movement depends on not colliding with others. Under that model, the human being is a thing that enters into a system that facilitates or obstructs its movement. Under this model, the human being is actually a *being*. An alternative model, shared by many groups across southern Africa, Asia, South America, and even parts of Continental Europe, is a relational version of the human being as part of a larger system of meaning. Actions, from that perspective, are not about whether "I" succeed but instead about "our" unending story across time. Under this model, no human being is a being *simpliciter* or being-in-her-or-himself-or-themselves. As relational, it means that each human being is a constant negotiation of ongoing efforts to build relationships with others, which means no one actually enters a situation without establishing new situations of action and meaning. Instead of entering a game, their participation requires a different kind of project—especially where the "game" was premised on their exclusion. Thus, where the system or game repels initial participation, such repulsion is a shift in the grammar of how the system functions, especially its dependence on obsequious subjects. Shifted and shifting energy afford alternatives. *Kinds* cannot be known before the actions that birthed them. Participation, understood in these terms, is never *in* games but acts of changing them.

Abstract as this sounds, it has much historical support. For example, Evelyn Simien, in her insightful political study *Historic Firsts*, examines the new set of relations established in the United States by Shirley Chisholm's and Jesse Jackson's U.S. presidential campaigns.[18] There would have been no President Barack Obama without such important predecessors affecting the demographics of voter participation. Simien intentionally focused on the most mainstream example of political life to illustrate this point. Though no exemplar of radicalism or revolution, Obama's "success" came from Chisholm and

Jackson's (and many others') so-called "failure." Despite the appalling reactionary response of a right-wing majority in the 114th Congress during the second term of Obama's presidency and the election of Donald Trump, whose obsession with erasing Obama's legacy exemplified a form of psychoanalytical little man's trauma, the historic fact remains that Obama took the helm of a mismanaged executive branch and gave it a level of dignity and intelligence matched by few of its white exemplars. His successors claim for a restored greatness only reveals the joke that is, in fact, any project on which the term "supremacy" is built: the naked racism and mediocrity that followed—there is an amusing photograph of a Klansman holding up a sign declaring his race's "superior *jeans!*"—reveal the folly and terror of white megalomania. Beyond presidential electoral politics, there are numerous examples of how prior, radical so-called "failures" transformed relationships that facilitated other kinds of outcome. The trail goes back to the Haitian Revolution, which offered a vision of Black sovereignty that garnered the full force of Euromodern colonial and racist alliances to stall, and back to every act of resistance from Nat Turner's Rebellion in the USA, Sharpe's in Jamaica, or Tula's in Curaçao, and so many other efforts for social transformation to come.[19]

In existential terms, then, many ancestors of the African diaspora embodied what Kierkegaard calls an existential paradox. All the evidence around them suggested failure and the futility of hope. They first had to make a movement of infinite resignation—that is, resigning themselves to their situation. Yet they must simultaneously *act* against that resignation. Kierkegaard, as we have seen, called this seemingly contradictory phenomenon "faith," but that concept relates more to a relationship with a transcendent, absolute being, which could only be established by a "leap," as there are no mediations or bridge to the Absolute whose distant is, as Kierkegaard put it, absolutely absolute. Ironically, if Afropessimism appeals to transcendent intervention, it would collapse into faith. If the Afropessimist's argument rejects transcendent intervention and focuses on committed political action, of taking responsibility for a future that offers no guarantees, then the movement from infinite resignation becomes existential political action.

At this point, the crucial meditation would be on politics and political action. An attitude of infinite resignation to the world without the leap of committed action would simply be pessimistic or nihilistic. Similarly, an attitude of hope or optimism about the future would lack infinite resignation. We see here the underlying failure of the two approaches. Yet ironically, there is a form of *failure at failing* in the pessimistic turn versus the optimistic one, since if focused exclusively on resignation as the goal, then the "act" of resignation would have been achieved, which, paradoxically, would be a success; it would be a successful failing of failure. For politics to emerge, there are two missing elements in inward pessimistic resignation to consider.

The first is that politics is a social phenomenon, which means it requires the expanding options of a social world. It must transcend the self. Turning *away* from the social world, though a statement *about* politics, is not in and of itself *political*. As we have seen, the ancients from whom much Western political theory or philosophy claimed affinity had a disparaging term for an individual resigned from political life—namely, *idiōtēs*, a private person, one not concerned with public affairs, in English: an idiot. I mention "Western political theory" because that is the hegemonic intellectual context of Afropessimism; I have not come across Afropessimistic writings on thought outside of that framework. We do not have to end our etymological journey in ancient Greek. Recall that extending our linguistic archaeology back a few thousand years we could examine the Middle Kingdom (2000 BCE–1700 BCE) of Kmt's Mdw Ntr word *idi* (deaf). The presumption, later taken on by the ancient Athenians and other Greek-speaking peoples, was that a lack of hearing entailed isolation, at least in terms of audio speech. The contemporary inward resignation of seeking a form of purity from the loathsome historical reality of racial oppression, in this reading, retreats ultimately into a form of moralism (private, normative satisfaction) instead of public responsibility born of and borne by action. The nonbeing to which Afropessimists refer is also a form of inaudibility.

The second is the importance of power. Politics makes no sense without it. As we have seen throughout our earlier reflections on power, Eurocentric etymology points to the Latin word *potis* as its source, from which came the word "potent" as in an omnipotent god. If we again look back farther, we will notice the Middle Kingdom Mdw Ntr word *pHty*, which refers to godlike strength. Yet for those ancient Northeast Africans, even the gods' abilities came from a source. In the *Coffin Texts*, *HqAw* or *heka* activates the *ka* (sometimes, as we have seen, translated as soul, spirit, womb, or "magic"), which makes reality.[20] All this amounts to a straightforward thesis on power as the ability with the means to make things happen.

There is an alchemical quality of power. The human world, premised on symbolic communication, brings many forms of meaning into being, and those new meanings afford relationships that build institutions through a world of culture, a phenomenon that Freud, we should recall, rightly described as "a prosthetic god." It is godlike because it addresses what humanity historically sought from the gods—protection from the elements, physical maledictions, and social forms of misery. Such power clearly can be abused. It is where those enabling capacities (empowerment) are pushed to the wayside in the hording of social resources into propping up some people as gods that the legitimating practices of cultural cum political institutions decline and stimulate pessimism and nihilism. The institutions in Abya Yala and in Northern countries, such as the United States and Canada, very rarely attempt to establish positive relations to blacks, and Blacks the subtext of Afropessimism and this entire meditation.

The discussion points to a demand for political commitment. Politics is manifested under different names throughout the history of our species, but the one occasioning the word "politics" is, as we have seen, from the Greek *pólis*, which refers to ancient Hellenic city-states. It identifies specific kinds of activities conducted *inside* the city-state, where order necessitated the resolution of conflicts through rules of discourse the violation of which could lead to (civil) war, a breaking down of relations into those appropriate for "outsiders." Returning to the Fanonian observation of selves and others, it is clear that imposed limitations on certain groups amount to impeding or blocking the option and activities of politics. Yet, as a problem occurring *within the polity*, the problem short of war becomes a political one.

Returning to Afropessimistic challenges, the question becomes this. If the problem of antiblack racism is conceded as political—where antiblack institutions of power have, as their project, the impeding of Black power, which in effect requires barring Black access to political institutions—then antiblack societies are ultimately threats also to politics defined as the human negotiation of the expansion of human capabilities or, more to the point, appearance, speech, and freedom.

Antipolitics is one of the reasons why societies in which antiblack racism is hegemonic are also those in which racial moralizing dominates; moralizing stops at individuals at the expense of addressing institutions the transformation of which would make immoral individuals irrelevant. As a political problem, it demands a political solution. It is not accidental that blacks continue to be the continued exemplars of unrealized freedom and against whom violence is waged against appearance and speech. As so many from Ida B. Wells-Barnett to Angela Y. Davis, Michelle Alexander, Angela J. Davis, Noël Cazenave have shown the expansion of privatization and incarceration is squarely placed in a structure of states and civil societies premised on the limitations of freedom (Blacks)—ironically, as seen in countries such as South Africa and the United States, *in the name of freedom*.[21]

That power is a facilitating or enabling phenomenon, a functional element of the human world, a viable response must be the establishment of relations that reach beyond the singularity of the body. I bring this up because proponents of Afropessimism might object to this analysis because of its appeal to a *human* world. If that world is abrogated, the site of struggle becomes that which is patently *not human*. It is not accidental that popular race discourse refers today to "black bodies" instead of "black people," for instance. As the human world is discursive, social, and relational, this abandonment amounts to an appeal to the nonrelational, the incommunicability of radicalized singularity, and appeals to the body and its very limited reach, if not isolation. At that point, it is perhaps the psychologist, psychiatrist, or psychoanalyst who would be helpful, as turning radically inward offers the promise of despair, narcissistic delusions of divine power, and, as Fanon also observed, madness.[22] Even if that slippery slope were rejected, the performative contradiction of attempting *to communicate* such singularity or absence thereof requires, at least for consistency, the appropriate course of action: silence.

The remaining question for Afropessimism, especially those who are primarily academics, becomes this: Why write?

It is a question for which, in both existential and political terms, I do not see how an answer could be given from an Afropessimistic perspective without the unfortunate revelation of cynicism. The marketability of Afropessimists in predominantly white institutions—perhaps as an exotic phenomenon that affirms white standpoints as ontological sites of legitimacy—is no doubt in the immediate and paradoxical satisfaction in dissatisfaction it offers. Indeed, if Afropessimists were correct, their only solace would be in black institutions, but that, too, would pose a problem since the argument is that such institutions lack agency because, as black, they are absent. This is not to say that critical black and Black thinkers should not do their work in predominantly white spaces. It is simply that the argument of the impossibility of their doing so makes their location in such places patently contradictory. We are at this point on familiar terrain. As with ancient logical paradoxes denying the viability of time and motion, the best option, after a moment of immobilized reflection, is, eventually, to move on, even where the pause is itself significant as an encomium of thought.

Notes

1. See, for example, Boulou Ebanda de B'béri and P. Eric Luow, "Afropessimism: A Genealogy of Discourse," *Critical Arts* 25, no. 3 (2011): 335–346; Sandra J. Schmidt and H. James Garrett, "Reconstituting Pessimistic Discourses," *Critical Arts* 25, no. 3 (2011): 423–440.

2. See, for example, Lewis R. Gordon, *Bad Faith and Antiblack Racism* (Atlantic Highlands, NJ: Humanities International Press, 1995), 25th anniversary edition 2021 with Humanities Classics, and *Existentia Africana: Understanding African Existential Thought* (New York, NY: Routledge, 2000).

3. Martin Heidegger, "Letter on Humanism," in *Basic Writings from "Being and Time" (1928) to "The Task of Thinking" (1964)*, ed. David F. Krell (San Francisco, NC: HarperSanFrancisco, 1971), 213–266. [Letter from 1947].

4. For example, Lewis R. Gordon, "Theory in Black: Teleological Suspensions in Philosophy of Culture," *Qui Parle: Critical Humanities and Social Sciences* 18, no. 2 (Spring/Summer 2010): 193–214 and, of course, the previous chapters of this collection.

5. See, for example, Keiji Nishitani, *Religion and Nothingness*, trans. Jan Van Bragt (Berkeley, CA: University of California Press, 1982 [1961]), 16.

6. See Matthew C. Eshleman and Constance L. Mui (eds.), *The Sartrean Mind* (London, UK; Routledge, 2020) for discussion from a full range of such theorists.

7. Daniel McNeil, "'Mixture Is a Neoliberal Good': Mixed-Race Metaphors and Post-Racial Masks," *Dark Matter* 9 no. 1 (2012): 3–16 and "Slimy Subjects and Neoliberal Goods: Obama and the Children of Fanon," *Journal of Critical Mixed Race Studies* 1.1 (2014): 203–218. See also David Marriott, *Wither Fanon?: Studies in the Blackness of Being* (Palo Alto, CA: Stanford University Press, 2018) and Calvin L. Warren, *Ontological Terror: Blackness, Nhilism, and Emancipation* (Durham, NC: Duke University Press, 2018).

8. For discussion of epistemic apartheid, see Reiland Rabaka, *Against Epistemic Apartheid: W.E.B. Du Bois and the Disciplinary Decadence of Sociology* (Lanham, MD: Lexington Books, 2010).

9. The most detailed effort to work out the implications of this position is Calvin Warren's *Ontological Terror*.

10. Frank Wilderson, III, "Biko and the Problematic Presence," in Amanda Alexander, Nigel Gibson, and Andile Mngxitama (eds.), *Biko Lives!: Contestations and Conversations* (New York, NY: Palgrave, 2008), 95–114.

11. Jared Sexton, "The Social Life of Social Death: On Afro-Pessimism and Black Optimism," In *Tensions Journal* 5 (Fall/Winter, 2011): 1–47.

12. Fanon does not elaborate this line of argumentation. I offer such in *What Fanon Said: A Philosophical Introduction to His Life and Thought* (New York, NY: Fordham University Press; London, UK: Hurst Publishers; Johannesburg, South Africa: Wits University Press, 2015).

13. For elaboration of these elements of *Peau noire, masques blancs* (Paris, France: Éditions du Seuil, 1952) and *Les Damnés de la terre* (Paris, France: François Maspero, 1961), see Lewis R. Gordon, *What Fanon Said: A Philosophical Introduction to His Life and Thought* (New York, NY: Fordham UP; London, UK: Hurst; Johannesburg, South Africa: Wits University Press, 2015).

14. *Peau noire, masques blancs*, 89.

15. See Frantz Fanon, *Sociologie d'une révolution: l'an V de la révolution algérienne*, 2nd edition (Paris, France: François Maspero, 1975 [1959]), available in English as *A Dying Colonialism*, trans. Haakon Chevalier (New York, NY: Grove Press, 1967).

16. For criticisms of other elements, see Devon R. Johnson, A Philosophical Analysis of Nihilism and Antiblack Racism (Temple University Doctoral Dissertation, 2014) ; Greg Thomas, "Afro-Blue Notes: The Death of Afro-pessimism (2.0)?," *Theory & Event* 21, no. 1 (January 2018): 282–317; and Dwayne Tunstall, "Curing Black Melancholia with Africana Philosophy," *American Institute of Philosophical and Cultural Thought* (18 September 2020): https://www.youtube.com/watch?v=owP3qumV06A.

17. See Friedrich Nietzsche, *On the Genealogy of Morals*, trans. Walter Kaufman and R.J. Holingdale (New York, NY: Vintage, 1967) and *Will to Power*, trans. Walter Kaufman and R.J. Hollingdale (New York, NY: Vintage, 1968).

18. Evelyn M. Simien, *Historic Firsts: How Symbolic Empowerment Changes U.S. Politics* (New York, NY: Oxford University Press, 2016).

19. For this understanding of sovereignty offered by the Haitian Revolution, see Jeremy Matthew Glick, *The Black Radical Tragic: Performance, Aesthetics, and the Unfinished Haitian Revolution* (New York, NY: New York University Press, 2016).

20. Adriaan de Buck and Alan H. Gardiner (eds.), *The Ancient Egyptian Coffin Texts. c. 2181–2055 BCE* (Chicago, IL: The University of Chicago Oriental Institute Publications Volume LXVII; University of Chicago Press, 1951).

21. Ida B. Wells-Barnett, *The Red Record: Tabulated Statistics and Alleged Causes of Lynching in the United States* (Scotts Valley, CA: CreateSpace Independent Publishing Platform, 2015 [1895]); Angela Y. Davis, *Are Prisons Obsolete?* (New York, NY: Seven Stories Press, 2003); Michelle Alexander, *The New Jim Crow: Mass Incarceration in the Age of Colorblindness* (New York, NY: Free Press, 2010); Angela J. Davis, *Arbitrary Justice: The Power of the American Prosecutor* (New York, NY: Oxford University Press, 2009); and Noël Cazenave's *Killing African Americans: Police Vigilante Violence as a Racial control Mechanism* (New York, NY: Routledge, 2018).

22. See Frantz Fanon, *Alienation and Freedom*, trans. Steven Corcoran (London, UK: Bloomsbury Academic, 2018), where he outlines these considerations in his psychiatric writings, and his letter of resignation from working as the head of Blida-Joinville Hospital in Algeria, published in Frantz Fanon, *Pour la revolution africaine: écrits politiques* (Paris, France: François Maspero, 1969), available in English through Grove Press as *Toward the African Revolution*, trans. Haakon Chevalier (1967).

Chapter 6

Emancipatory Challenges of Blackness

"Race," as the novelist and literary theorist Sylvia Wynter argues, is also a "biodicy."[1] By this, she means that the theodicean grammar of the world in which race was constituted is also, we should understand, one about the negotiation of life and death. Among its many consequences, race is about in one sense who lives and who dies. In another sense, its normative significance leads to a rephrasing of who is *supposed* to live and who to die.[2]

Theodicy, we should recall, literally means "gods' justice." From *theo* (god) and *dikē* (often translated as "justice"), the word comes from a problem forged by expectations of a good or benevolent, omniscient, and omnipotent deity. Such a being is presumed committed to what is right—in some reasoning even more, where the Being itself is what is right and good—which makes the emergence of evil and injustice a major problem. If the deity has the capacity to eradicate evil, indeed, the ability to have prevented its emergence in the first place, why is there so much evil and injustice in the world?

The problem raises a variety of vexing problems for all except perhaps the most extraordinary of the faithful or the most naïve among them. If the deity's benevolence is a necessary condition of its existence, then the presence of iniquity suggests either the deity's impotence or malicious foreknowledge. If evil and injustice are the deity's will, the universe is under the yoke of a very bad or at least sadistic deity. Another conclusion is simply that the deity does not exist.

A third solution is to demonstrate the compatibility of evil and injustice alongside the existence of such a god. Many theologians have taken this course. From Saint Augustine of Hippo in the 4th century through early 5th century through to Gottfried Wilhelm Leibniz in the 17th century through early 18th century and Kwame Gyekye, John Hicks, William R. Jones, Sherman Jackson, and Anthony Pinn in recent times, the conundrum persists with answers not often satisfactory for the faithful.[3] Not much has gone beyond Saint Augustine's reflection on two exonerating conditions for his deity, although argued in many instances with increasing brilliance, which was for his fellow Christians and him *the* Deity: the problem is a consequence of human limitations.

Human beings are not omniscient and therefore cannot possibly understand the full significance of what *appears* to be evil and unjust. That familiar response boils down to the old adage, "G-d knows."[4] The alternative response reminds us of the significance of love. The deity endowed humanity with free will. As an act of love, it demands restraint as human will, imperfect as it is, makes its way through the ages through actions good and bad, right and wrong. In both formulations, human beings are the problem. Gyekye, Jones, and Pinn are, while endorsing its humanistic ethical implications, not satisfied with this response.[5] Its metaphysical implications are not in favor of the deity's existence.

Others, such as Friedrich Wilhelm Joseph Schelling, G.W.F. Hegel, and Friedrich Nietzsche had thought through the implications of theodicy at the level of nature and history.[6] The existential problem raises the question of what is permitted to be in the world versus what is not. If the unfolding of time and history is at the end of the day "right," then what is to be made of that which it eliminates and those who are pushed to the wayside in this drama? They, along with others such as W.E.B. Du Bois through to Frantz Fanon and more, have noticed the continued presence of this kind of argumentation even where there is the absence of an avowed deity.[7] Even secular societies may have a theodicean mode of rationalization, where the society itself or some system of treasured knowledge or values occupies the deific role. In theology, this is called idolatry.

For our purposes, idolatry offers a theodicean grammar or form. Its rationalization depends on rendering its contradictions *external*, which means, from a systemic point of view, being systematically "dead." This dimension of theodicy, then, shifts as normative investment moves from knowledge and society to life, from biology (*bio-logos*) to a biodicy (*life-justice*). We could call this the presupposition of inherently lived justification.

Such is not only the story of race but also the specificity of its Euromodern, Manichean manifestation. That proto-race had its origin in theological naturalism brings these considerations to the fore. The world of theological naturalism was, after all, one in which the theological and the natural were inseparable. There was no supernatural in that world because the natural was that which was the deity produced. Thus, instead of the natural and the supernatural, primary distinctions in Euromodernity, there was the natural and the unnatural. The latter simply meant that which deviated from the former. In Medieval Christian theology, the unnatural was that which deviated from Christ, which made it also evil or demonic. Among such deviations were two refusing groups—Jews and Muslims.

The etymology of "race" points to this theological naturalism but with odd considerations. The proto-term was *raza*, which referred to breeds of dogs, horses and then Jews and Moors.[8] The complicated issue with dogs and horses, as we know, is that their development from their ancestral species was through human involvement. Thus, their "natural" form was heavily mediated or, under another interpretation, deviated through domestication. It would be odd to consider dogs and horses "unnatural," however. That they are domesticated animals signals a relationship between them and the human beings whom they serve. This is no doubt why animals are often more revered than people in racist societies. They are ultimately "natural." Jews and Moors, on the other hand, represented a deviation from the natural; each supposedly once part of divine creation, they are, nevertheless, deviations through supposedly human hubris. Comparing them with domesticated animals, then, signaled also the social role they were expected ultimately to play in a schema where the natural was reintroduced. Thus, in the "Reconquest" of Christendom, a term referring more to an order of power and process of purging than to historical fact—since there was not a prior Christian conquest of Islam because the latter emerged after Christianity and was, in fact, the conqueror (perhaps liberator for the pagans)—the search for signs, markings of unnatural origins was among its governing activities well attested to by the Inquisition, which was formally conducted from the 12th through the early 16th centuries, although it continued in less dramatic form through to the 19th century.[9]

The question of origins was among the considerations of *raza*. For the term was not in its origins Germanic, Latin, or Greek, languages that dominated the northern Mediterranean, but instead Arabic, Hebrew, and ancient Egyptian or Mdw Ntr. As a variation of such words as *ra'* (Arabic), *rosh* (Hebrew), and *ra* (Mdw Ntr), words referring to "head," "beginning," and "sun," its significance for origins was clear. The sun, after all, rises in the east and sets in the west. The Afro-Muslim conquest of Iberia, which created Andalusia, no doubt offered distinctions premised on origins—a consideration not only among the conquered Christians but also among the Muslims who were transformed, the more their faith reached beyond West Asia westward to where the Atlantic Ocean and Mediterranean Sea met.[10]

The Christian triumph in Grenada in 1492 meant, among many things, the expansion of a legitimation crisis, where origins became a constant consideration even as ships reached shores in which those who greeted them were not Christian, Jew, or Muslim. The epistemic upheavals that followed, where justification shifted from the deity to the question of deities themselves, where accounting for the natural required nontheological sources, led to new examinations of origins and correlative anthropologies; *raza* was adopted, adapted, and transformed into classification systems through which, over time, race was born. But along with this transformation were also continued forms of rationalization. Thus, as deviance was marked by a shift from normative centers, old, theologically symbolic markers of the Light and the Dark, Manichean throughout, continued. There was no hope of a good deal for the Night in this tale.[11]

The historical situation of the dark, which eventually became the black, was marked before the 16th century debates between Bartolomé de las Casas and Juan Ginés de Sepúlveda about the humanity of Indigenous populations of Abya Yala (the Americas) and their salvation both spiritually and biologically through appeal to heathenish and darker sources from Africa.[12] The "Reconquest" had already set the stage for the relationship with the black, but this blackness was one in which refuge could not be sought in the soul because of its already betrayed presence in the color of such people's skin. To make matters worse, the populations marked by blackness had no reason to have expected such, which meant their inauguration into this schema, an epidermal one as Frantz Fanon characterized it in *Black Skin, White Masks*, was without knowledge of the logic that erased their inner or lived reality. A form of amnesia was necessary to transform people from a world in which they once saw themselves as the future—as, in other words, their version of modern—to the Fanonian problematic near the end of *The Damned of the Earth*: "In reality, what am I?"[13]

This problematic of blackness is symbiotically linked to the world in which Christendom was transformed into Europe, where Germanic and Mediterranean Christians were transformed into whites. As there was neither reason to have considered themselves black nor African prior to the impositions of these identities on them from kidnapping to Middle Passage to enslavement, African diasporic existence as black became marked by the peculiarity of paradox and melancholic displacement.[14] The former was a consequence of having to have always been what one becomes. The melancholia is to be endemic to a world in which one is rejected—to be homeless in the epoch to which one is indigenous. Paradoxes abound through displacement at levels of identity, for to be black is not to be; it is paradoxically "to be," as Fanon observed, in the zone of nonbeing. Thus, blackness is fundamental to the formation of European modernity as one that imagines itself legitimate and pure through the expurgation of blackness. It is, in other words, a function of the theodicy of European modernity.

W.E.B. Du Bois saw this problem in many ways. In one sense, he formulated it as the problem of being a problem. This realization led to a schism in which consciousness of society and of not belonging to it through paradoxically being endemic to it is one of his great insights. He outlined well the theodicean problematic of blackness as the absent term, even in its presence. This logic required apartheid behavior even at epistemic levels, as Railand Rybalka correctly observed, and that consideration moved more radically to the conditions for the possibility of thought itself.[15] In effect, it demanded purification of theory, which meant theory that behaves, theory that abides by the rules, theory, in other words, with limited vision. The reference to vision is no accident here, as the word "theory," comes to us etymologically from the Greek infinitive *theorein* ("to see"), through which we get *theoria*. As with *theodicy*, the theological groundings of this concept should be evident, which reminds us of a basic insight of theoretical work as an attempt to see what deities would see. To see as a god would be an extraordinary achievement for humanity, which is no doubt why much of early Euromodern reflection on decoding the universe took the form of deciphering the language of, in monotheism, G-d. Where G-d is seen as light, there is no darkness, which makes all truth, all thought, ultimately without contradiction. Truth and thought obey G-d in this theological metaphysics precisely because such a deity could command their obedience. In that conception, necessity and sufficiency meet because thought and deed, from that which is omniscient and omnipotent, are one. We should, as we have been seeing, be cautious about seeking contemporary epistemic terms only in their Greco and Latin past. The word *theoria*, after all, is a conjunction of two words—*thea* and *horan*—the latter of whose origin is not Greek. The first refers to view, and is, as should be obvious, linked to what we know today as "theater." The second, which today is connected to the word "aura," is properly linked to the Hebrew word *"or"* ("to become light"). As with many conceptually rich terms, we see here a meeting of words through that of worlds. The proverbial plot thickens when one extends the connection to theater. Despite beings seated to view what is on the stage, nothing happens until it is lit. Du Bois's raising the problem of being a problem has resonance when one considers being seated in a theater in which certain members of the cast remain behind the curtains. Although the stage is lit, no light shines upon them and the characters they play can be referred to but never properly seen and, worse, never see. No light shines from their faces. They are, despite being on the stage, absent in plain sight. They might as well be, in Du Bois's language, behind the veil. Such a practice requires rules of exclusion.

Epistemic theodicy takes the form of demanding the supervenience of consistency models of rationality and knowledge premised on exclusion. In effect, it requires demanding reason's obedience as a practice of erasure. A problem surfaces when the scope of this effort includes its own evaluation. It begs the question for rationality to assess its own consistency, since it is consistency itself that is up for evaluation. To evaluate consistency or rationality requires something more and that is *reason*. What, in other words, if reason does not behave? And what if its delinquency is precisely because, as an evaluator, it must be above, paradoxically, even itself? These kinds of questions reveal the contradictions of metasystems, of any theoretical model capable of self-evaluation. But brought down to earth in the context of these reflections, it means addressing the sides of theory that rationality hoped to suppress, and what are they other than their darker sides? Theory, in other words, could only articulate the light because its reach is also into its negations—namely, the zones of nonbeing.[16] Put differently, if there were no darkness amid the light on the stage, nothing can be seen.

This understanding leads to rethinking some key features of the emergence of colonized epistemic practices. To identify them as colonized means to admit their suppressed terms, their hidden or feared undersides. The previous meditations on theory bring to the fore considerations of practices of science as well. Here, we are in a terrain similar to our earlier reflections from Du Bois to Paget Henry to Jane Anna Gordon on potentiated double consciousness, where the contradictions of false particularities unveil and enlarge the grammatical practices of knowledge—in more prosaic language, the universalizing, as opposed to universal, activities of expanding thought.[17] And made plainer, this means blackness, broader in scope, unmasks the false security of whiteness. Reality, in other words, is always bigger than that.

Among the many instances of this unfolding is the constellation of epistemic practices known as the human sciences. One fallacy is the tendency to treat these sciences as "pure," wherein their completeness is demonstrated and then they are methodically "applied" to human beings.[18] What is missing is the understanding that such sciences are generated out of what people do and their focused subject, "human being," was already racially inflected during the formation of those sciences through the presupposition of epistemic practices premised on normative whiteness. The human sciences were generated, after all, out of the question, "What is man?"[19] But as we have seen that question emerged through encounters with the extraordinary and the different. It is when a presumed human "we" meets "them," interrogation follows on the question of whether "we" are "they." This rupture leads to meditations on the question of standards by which "we" are determined as who or what we are and "they" are the same for what they are. This identity question leads to further meditations on those standards, and in them is the additional problem of defining human being.[20] This philosophical anthropological question, if we will, is rendered more difficult by the epistemic upheavals that erupted from a collapsed theological naturalism. Where necessity no longer reins as a god, where "idea" does not mean existence, where the human being must take hold of the responsibility of what is seen (secular theory), the possibility of what to become is transformed into the metaphysical and epistemic investment in no less than the problem of *freedom* in an epoch conditioned through and through by the presupposition of racial difference. In blackness, in other words, there are three conditions of modern thought itself under the weight of Euromodernity—namely, philosophical anthropology, freedom, and the justificatory practices of both.[21]

The emergence of the first is already outlined and understood through the historical reality of systems denying the humanity of whole groups of human beings in the first place. Such denial, contradictory in terms (because relying on the supposed nonhumanity of some human groups, of putting outside of human relations that which depends upon human relationships), inevitably leads to the effort to force behavior on human subjects through epistemic and political acts of closure. The problem is that a closed human being, a human being without possibility, is not a human being.[22] Freedom, then, became an intimate condition of human exemplification. As symbiotic, the two generate legitimating questions and, thus, the justificatory practice—is blackness justifiable?[23] I have elsewhere called this the metacritique of reason precisely because of the black side of thought premised on contradictions of reason.[24] A Fanonian allegory is perhaps useful here. Recall that in the fifth chapter of *Black Skin, White Masks*, Fanon observed the flight of reason when the Black enters the room. The Black could "force" reason's obedience, but this will no doubt be unreasonable. But reason's flight as he reached out to it is also unreasonable. The Black faces, in other words, as we have seen, the nightmare of unreasonable reason. Barred from the use of force, the only alternative is to reason with such (unreasonable) reason.[25] This reasoning, if we will, is the continued burden of blackness.

These reflections pertain fundamentally to the epistemic challenges of blackness. I do not, however, think they are radical enough. One presupposition of decolonizing the epistemic conditions is that there will be a form of normative catharsis. The presumption is that a form of false *knowledge* is sequestering the kinds of responsible activities needed to think and act better, and by the latter I mean at least ethically and justly. These normative terms are often presumed as prisoners behind European-nurtured epistemic walls. What if there were another layer of imprisonment? What if the presumed normative resources to be unleashed from putting aside epistemic infelicities persist at a more radical level—that is, as we have seen in our earlier meditations on justice, at those of the norms themselves?

In his critique of European colonialism, Aimé Césaire raised a similar concern when he argued that what transpired in World War II was not anomalous but instead a manifestation of the actual values Europeans lived in the colonies—namely, "Hitlerism."[26] It was not only that European colonialism actively fought against the humanity of colonized subjects but also that the modes or technologies of colonization were also expressions of Europe itself. The fascism expressed in the actions of Hitler is what black people under white rule have been living for around 500 years. That being the case, Césaire's analysis of what emerged on the European continent was simply its value system turned inward. His argument was not that there were no good things about Europe. As a human community, it also had bad elements, and as those were pushed outward to the colonies (in theodicean language, outside of the god), they eventually spilled over into a vengeful return.

Césaire identified a problem later echoed by Fanon in his urging for people of what is today called the Global South to look beyond Europe for inspiration and develop new concepts and set afoot a new humanity. The conceptual question alerts us to the epistemic challenge, but Fanon's praxis-demand ("set afoot" a new humanity) speaks to a task at the level of lived reality. Even more, Fanon earlier in the same step encouraged going beyond the "Greco-Latin" or Greek and Roman pedestal of European values.[27] While proponents of those values might attempt to defend them as *human values* or *universal values*, this normative critique questions this assertion on a par with that of double consciousness and potentiated double consciousness. Is it not another case of European particularity asserting itself as human universality? And even more, as we saw in the philosophical anthropological question, is not part of a radical critique the critical question of the privileging of one group of human beings as *the* human in the first place?

We are on familiar terrain. As with the theological and epistemic questions, the normative one faces the problem of theodicean grammar as well. Are the norms for which many of us are fighting in the name of, say, racial justice or liberation from antiblack racism free of normative colonization even where they may be so at an epistemic level? Is it not presumptuous to think that the decolonization of knowledge has the same for norms as its consequence?

We do already have a clue on this potentially vexing problem. Blackness, after all, as the underside of theory, is a relational concept.[28] To think of blackness means always to imagine it in relation to something else since to do so is to establish at least a phenomenological relationship of thought to its object or subject.[29] This basic relationship offers the critique of the theodicean one, where the role of a god in effect eliminates the rest of the world by becoming an exclusive domain. It requires being without an outside and, thus, being *outside of relations with anything else.* The distinction of being-in-relations versus non-relationality raises a normative difference since blackness, and its relationship not only to the included but also to the excluded, promises an ever-widening normative range. One may object that this observation pertains as well to whiteness, since it would be rendered incoherent as a concept without nonwhiteness. But we should bear in mind that the argument here is that whiteness is invested with notions of purity and exclusion. Delusional as this may be, it is part of the reality of how whiteness is lived. It thus, continuing the delusion, is sustained through the persistence of misguided problematics, as seen in Immanuel Kant's philosophical anthropology, the notion of difference as deviation.[30] The "origin" in his thought is presumed to be pure and white, and radical deviation becomes adulterated and black. What should be obvious from the relational analysis conducted thus far is that the proper question is not about how difference came into being but, instead, how purity became the model of origin. After all, origination requires relationship to something else, and most at least biological nature reveals origins of species and genera from sites of maximum diversity instead of purity. Purity, in other words, despite its proponents' protestations, also signals deviation—namely, one from initial difference and diversity.

Normative antipathy to difference is not only at the heart of avowed descriptive or normative-free science but also, as we have been seeing, in normative theorizing of normativity wedded to such thought. Recall our earlier discussion of what we could call "justice talk." This activity is, as we saw, often done as if it were all-encompassing but insufficiently addressed. Thus, there is always the search for justice as though every normative arrangement of social institutions has simply fallen short of its virtue, as John Rawls had espoused through his claim of justice as the primary virtue of institutions.[31] This presumption works, of course, if justice were simply a term already present in every human community and simply stand within the Northern European tradition of thought as a term translatable into its correlates or instantiations in other languages. But translatability often begs many important questions of human difference. It could not only be the case, as we saw in our earlier discussion of John Rawls, that "justice" was not translated but in fact imposed on other languages and societies. It could also be that the scope of the word "justice," even where translatable, is part of a smaller normative field within the framework of the non-European groups onto whom it is posed. If this is correct, then the proponent of justice has the task not only of understanding what is common about conceptions of justice across human communities, but also what could be learned beyond justice across them as well. Where justice is asserted in a theodicean way, this is a terrifying thought, as it requires looking at the underside of justice only as "injustice" instead of what may be "right" or "good," as we have seen, *beyond justice*.[32]

Race, theodicy, and normativity, then, pose special questions for our age, especially in terms of challenges raised by blackness. The last, for instance, has a bad habit of demonstrating societal, scientific, and normative contradictions. Blackness, constantly posed as illicit appearance, means that hopes for justice in a system premised on licit appearance leads not only to contradictions but also to the maintenance of exclusion *in the name of justice*. In the realm of science, there was the presumption that science is correctly implemented through the exclusion of race, particularly blackness. The critique is the same as on the societal level. It is a theodicy that elides the symbiotic foundation of its own system. The human sciences, for instance, emerged out of worries and encounters with human difference. Instead of bad human science producing race, it was, in other words, race that produced human science, since it required a meditation not only on the human but also *the really human*. I have outlined some of the normative problematics in terms of justice, but there is more to consider, for the normative dimensions of what it means to be human also affect the conditions of appearance and other norms such as those of violation and violence. If one is not supposed to appear, then one has violated a norm simply by doing so.[33]

Blackness, then, is a challenge at the heart of what is to be done as humanity reflects on how it is bound to its subsequent generations—how, that is, it is bound to itself. This binding, the hallmark of religiosity, raises the question as well, in an avowed secular age, of the extent to which religiosity itself as a disavowed condition is also a blackened one. These reflections at levels of knowledge and value, the separation of which we have seen neither to be neat or even viable, should be of some use as we continue to reflect on the continued significance and future of things black.

Notes

1. Sylvia Wynter, "On How We Mistook the Map for the Territory, and Re-Imprisoned Ourselves in 'Our Unbearable Wrongness of Being,' of Désêtre: Black Studies toward the Human Project," in Lewis R. Gordon and Jane Anna Gordon (eds.), *Not Only the Master's Tools: African-American Studies in Theory and Practice* (New York, NY: Routledge, 2006), 142.
2. This is familiar to anyone who reflects on racism and genocide. For critical discussion in these terms, see Ellen K. Feder, *Disciplining the Family* (New York, NY: Oxford University Press, 2008); Falguni Sheth, *Toward a Political Philosophy of Race* (Albany, NY: State University of New York Press, 2009); Lynne Tirrell, "Genocidal Language Games," in Ishani Maitra and Mary Kate McGowan (eds.), *Speech and Harm: Controversies over Free Speech* (Oxford, UK: Oxford University Press, 2012), 174–221.
3. See Saint Augustine, *The City of God*, trans. Marcus Doas, with an introduction by Thomas Merton (New York, NY: Modern Library, 1950); Gottfried Wilhelm Leibniz, *Theodicy*, trans. E.M. Huggard (New Haven, CT: Yale UP, 1952); Kwame Gyekye, *An Essay on African Philosophical Thought: The Akan Conceptual Scheme*, Revised Edition (Philadelphia, PA: Temple University Press, 1987); John Hicks's *Evil and the God of Love*, Revised Edition (New York, NY: Harper & Row, 1978); *Is God a White Racist: A Preamble to Black Theology*, 2nd Edition (Boston, MA: Beacon Press, 1997); Sherman A. Jackson, *Islam and Black Suffering* (New York, NY: Oxford University Press, 2009); and Anthony B. Pinn, *Why, Lord?: Suffering and Evil in Black Theology* (New York, NY: Continuum, 1999). See also Lewis R. Gordon, *An Introduction to Africana* Philosophy, 2nd Edition (Cambridge, UK: Cambridge University Press, 2021).
4. For readers wondering about this expression ("G-d"), the answer: I'm in the Jewish camp and subscribe to the logic of what is involved, including the hubris, of referring to the ineffable or, at least, that which shouldn't be fully written or uttered.
5. See Jones, *Is God a White Racist?*; Jackson, *Islam and Black Suffering*; and Pinn *Why Lord?* See also Lewis R. Gordon, "Theology and the Problem of African American History," in Katie G. Cannon and Anthony B. Pinn (eds.), *The Oxford Handbook of African American Theology* (New York, NY: Oxford University Press, 2014), 363–76.
6. For discussion, see, for example, Markus Gabriel, *Transcendental Ontology: Essays on German Idealism* (New York, NY: Continuum, 2011) and Slavoj Žižek and Markus Gabriel, *Mythology, Madness, and Laughter: Subjectivity in German Idealism* (New York, NY: Continuum, 2009).
7. See W.E.B. Du Bois, *The Souls of Black Folk: Essays and Sketches Chicago* (Chicago, IL: A.C. McClurg and Co., 1903) and Frantz Fanon, *Les Damnés de la terre* (Paris, France: Éditions Gallimard, 1991 [1961]), which I refer to as *The Damned of the Earth*. For discussion, see "Philosophical Anthropology, Race, and the Political Economy of Disenfranchisement," *The Columbia Human Rights Law Review* 36, no. 1 (Fall 2004): 145–72, *An Introduction to Africana Philosophy*, and *What Fanon Said: A Philosophical Introduction to His Life and Thought* (New York, NY: Fordham University Press; London, UK: Hurst Publishers; Johannesburg, South Africa: Wits University Press, 2015).
8. See Sebastian de Covarrubias Orozsco, who in his *Tesoro de la lengua* (1611), explained the term as pertaining to "the caste of purebred horses, which are marked by a brand so that they can be recognized. Raza in lineages is meant negatively, as in having some raza of Moor or Jew," quoted and trans. in David Nirenberg, "Race and the Middle Ages: The Case of Spain and Its Jews," in Margaret R. Greer, Walter D. Mignolo, and Maureen Quiligan (eds.), *Rereading the Black Legend: The Discourses of Religious and Racial Difference in the Renaissance Empires* (Chicago, IL: University of Chicago Press, 2007), 79.

9. Books on this historical system of investigations and trials. In addition to *Rereading the Black Legend*, see also Lamonte Aidoo's *Slavery Unseen: Sex, Power, and Violence in Brazilian History* (Durham, NC: Duke University Press, 2019).

10. Literature on this subject is vast. In addition to Mignolo et al, *Reading the Black Legend*, see Walter Mignolo, *The Darker Side of the Renaissance: Literacy, Territoriality, and Colonization*, 2nd Edition (Ann Arbor, MI: University of Michigan Press, 2003); Robert Davis, *Christian Slaves, Muslim Masters: White Slavery in the Mediterranean, the Barbary Coast and Italy, 1500–1800* (New York, NY: Palgrave Macmillan, 2003); and Ivan Van Sertima (ed.), *Golden Age of the Moor* (New Brunswick, Canada: Transaction Publishers, 1992). See also Lewis R. Gordon, *An Introduction to Africana Philosophy*, Chapter 1.

11. In addition to Lewis R. Gordon, *An Introduction to Africana Philosophy*, see also *Bad Faith and Antiblack Racism*, 2nd Edition (London, UK: Humanity Books, 2021); Eulalio Baltazar, *The Dark Center: A Process Theology of Blackness* (New York, NY: Paulist Press, 1973); Mignolo's *Darker Side of the Renaissance* and *The Darker Side of Western Modernity: Global Futures, Decolonial Options* (Durham, NC: Duke University Press, 2012); Nelson Maldonado-Torres, *Against War: Views from the Underside of Modernity* (Durham, NC: Duke University Press, 2008).

12. See Lewis Hanke, *All Mankind Is One: A Study of the Disputation Between Bartolomé De Las Casas and Juan Gines De Sepulveda in 1550 on the Intellectual and Religious Capacity* (Chicago, IL: Northern Illinois University Press, 1974).

13. See the penultimate chapter of *The Damned of the Earth*.

14. For elaboration along similar lines, see Nathalie Etoke, *Melancholia Africana: The Indispensable Overcoming of the Black Condition*, trans. Bill Hamlett (London, UK: Rowman and Littlefield International, 2019).

15. See Railand Rybalka, *Against Epistemic Apartheid: W.E.B. Du Bois and the Disciplinary Decadence of Sociology* (Lanham, MD: Lexington Books, 2010); cf. Lewis R. Gordon, *Disciplinary Decadence: Living Thought in Trying Times* (New York, NY: Routledge, 2006).

16. For more, see Lewis R. Gordon, "Theory in Black."

17. In addition to Du Bois's *Souls of Black Folk*, see Paget Henry, "Africana Phenomenology: Its Philosophical Implications," in Paget Henry, Jane Anna Gordon, Lewis R. Gordon, Aaron Kamugisha, and Neil Roberts (eds.), *Journeys in Caribbean Thought: The Paget Henry Reader* (London, UK: Rowman & Littlefield International, 2016), 27–58; Jane Anna Gordon, "The Gift of Double Consciousness: Some Obstacles to Grasping the Contributions of the Colonized," in Nalini Persram (ed.), *Postcolonialism and Political Theory* (Lanham, MD: Lexington Books, 2007), 143–161, and in *Creolizing Political Theory: Reading Rousseau through Fanon* (New York, NY: Fordham University Press, 2014).

18. For discussion of this fallacy, see Lewis R. Gordon, *Existentia Africana*, Chapter 4: "What Does It Mean to be a Problem?" Jane Anna Gordon, "Some Reflections on Challenges Posed to the Social Scientific Study of Race"; and Rybalka, *Against Epistemic Apartheid*.

19. See Michel Foucault, *The Order of Things: An Archaeology of the Human Sciences*, trans. Alan Sheridan (New York, NY: Vintage, 1994), for a magisterial study of this question and the formation of the human sciences, and see Sylvia Wynter, "On How We Mistook the Map for the Territory, and Re-Imprisoned Ourselves in 'Our Unbearable Wrongness of Being,' of Désêtre: Black Studies toward the Human Project," and B. Anthon Bogues (ed.), *After Man, Towards the Human: Critical Essays on the Thought of Sylvia Wynter* (Kingston, JA: Ian Randle, 2006).

20. For more, see Lewis R. Gordon, "Race in the Dialectics of Culture," in Abdul JanMohamed (ed.), *Reconsidering Social Identification: Race, Gender, Class and Caste* (New Delhi, India: Routledge India, 2011), 55–79.

21. See Lewis R. Gordon, "Theory in Black: Teleological Suspensions in Philosophy of Culture," *Qui Parle: Critical Humanities and Social Sciences* 18, no. 2 (Spring/Summer 2010): 193–214, and *An Introduction to Africana Philosophy*.

22. For more, see the discussion of epistemic closure in Lewis R. Gordon, *Fanon and the Crisis of European Man*, 2nd Edition (New York, NY: Routledge, 2021), Chapter 3.

23. See, for example, Lewis R. Gordon, *Existentia Africana: Understanding Africana Existential Thought* (New York, The Netherlands: Routledge, 2000), Chapter 1.

24. See Gordon, "Theory in Black."

25. See Lewis R. Gordon, "When Reason Is in a Bad Mood: A Fanonian Philosophical Portrait," in Hagi Kenaan and Illit Ferbert (eds.), *Philosophy's Moods: The Affective Grounds of Thinking* (Dordrecht, The Netherlands: Springer Press, 2011), 185–198.

26. Aimé Césaire, *Discourse on Colonialism*, trans. Joan Pinkham, with an introduction by Robin D. G. Kelley (New York, NY: Monthly Review Press, 2000), 41. See also Nelson Maldonado-Torres, *Against War*, Chapter 1: "From Liberalism to Hitlerism: Tracing the Origins of Violence and War," 23–51.

27. See *The Damned of the Earth*, the first chapter and conclusion. For discussion, see Lewis R. Gordon, "Fanon on Decolonizing Knowledge" in Elizabeth A. Hope and Tracey Nicholls (eds.), *Fanon and the Decolonization of Philosophy*, with a foreword by Mireille Fanon-Mendès-France (Lanham, MD: Lexington Books, 2010), 3–18 and *What Fanon Said: A Philosophical Introduction to His Life and Thought*. See also Elsa Dorlin, *Se défendre: une philosophie de la violence* (Paris, France: La Découverte, 2017).

28. See Gordon, "Theory in Black."

29. See "Theory in Black" and Lewis R. Gordon, "Black Existence in Philosophy of Culture," *Diogenes* 59, nos. 3–4 (2012): 96–105.

30. Kant is alone with this mentality, which persists into contemporary discourses of origins. For a compilation of misguided thinking on this subject from François Bernier to Kant through to Francis Galton, see Robert Bernasconi and Tommy Lott (eds.), *The Idea of Race* (Indianapolis, IN: Hackett Publishers, 2000). For a critical discussion of Kant's attitude to darkness, especially dark skin, see J. Reid Miller, *Stain Removal: Ethics and Race* (New York: Oxford University Press, 2016).

31. See Rawls's introduction to *A Theory of Justice* (Cambridge, MA: Harvard University Press, 1971).

32. See Chapter 3 of this volume. See also Mogobe Ramose offers a genealogy of normative bases of this phenomenon at the heart of Christian rationalizations of conquest and colonization in "Justice and Restitution in African Political thought," in P.H. Coetzee and A.P.J. Rous (eds.), *The African Philosophy Reader: A Text with Readings*, 2nd Edition (London, UK: Routledge, 2003), see 541–640, and Lewis R. Gordon, "Justice Otherwise: Thoughts on *Ubuntu*," in Leonhard Praeg (ed.), *Ubuntu: Curating the Archive* (Scottsville, South Africa: University of KwaZulu Natal Press, 2014), 10–26.

33. See, for example Lewis R. Gordon, "Below Even the Other: Colonialism's Violent Legacy and Challenge, with Respects to Fanon," *TransEuropeennes: International Journal of Critical Thought* (3 September 2012): http://www.transeuropeennes.eu/en/articles/358 and *Fear of Black Consciousness* (New York, NY: Farrar, Straus and Giroux; London, UK: Penguin Press, 2021), and Elsa Dorlin, *Se défendre*.

Chapter 7

Irreplaceability

> Existenz … is irreducibly in another; it is the absolutely firm, the irreplaceable, and therefore, as against all mere empirical existence, consciousness as such, and spirit, it is authentic being before Transcendence to which alone it surrenders itself without reservation.
>
> —Karl Jaspers[1]

Jaspers thinks of the human condition from a vantage point that, in today's world of thought subordinated by naturalism on the one hand and historicism on the other, might as well be of another world. According to Jaspers, there are limits that mark the horizon beyond which we are always, paradoxically, haunted not only by what has been, but also what is to come. The world that has followed, our world, is one in which nothing is sacred—except, perhaps, the idolatrous notion of The Market—the result of which is a seeming "limitlessness." The consequences of such a way of living are severe. Even the human being has become not much more than a cheap commodity. Thinking through the human, even in this period of the *post*human, then, is among the most important projects where we no doubt sit by the receding shores of ever-encroaching seas. What, we may ask, is the meaning of our condition if it is, in the end, replaceable? Given the peculiarly existential tone of this question, let us go through a series of existential explorations of what it might signify while seeking some guidance from Jaspers and several other important luminaries along the way.

Questioning Human Conditions

The question of the human in existential thought centers on the philosophical dimension of a being who, from the standpoint of natural science, is irritatingly unstable. Philosophy of existence is, as a *philosophy* seeks to render under the light of reason those opaque forces that once seemed beyond its scope and power. In that respect, philosophy, as many of us know, runs perilously close—wonderfully so in the eyes of some philosophers—to resembling science, wherein the search for "laws" of nature holds within it the conviction of Nature's ultimate limits. With philosophy comes the philosopher, and in our world, that curious being is situated in the realm of human being, which, to make matters difficult, is not properly being. Thus, the power of reason faces its own limitation in the form of the ever-transcending potential of the questioning questioner.

The ability to raise questions places the possibility of negation into the relation of thought, for the response called for is not simply a matter of truth or falsehood—not all questions require, that is, a yes or no answer. For questions, the possibilities range from assent to refusal, to approbation or rejection, to explanation or a gesture of indecision; in short, there is also the *value*-potential, often manifested by action, of responses. This development brings with it a peculiar dimension of the questioner's role, even where self-referential. Peter Caws states this dimension thus:

> Science is a kind of knowledge, and as such it must always be retrospective. But values are different from knowledge. They do not come to us from the world; they go from us to the world.[2]

We see here, then, the heart of two different views of producing knowledge. One view can be compared to lighting a match to light a candle to find one's way to a light switch to light a room. If the universe is the room, then science is the process of finding and turning on the successive switches and looking at what the spread of light reveals. Another view can be compared to the cosmological Big Bang itself, where knowledge is an ever-expanding reality spawned by an explosion—or, more accurately, a cooling of energy into matter. From this view, the very process of inquiry is not only a discovery but also *a production*. This makes knowledge a creative process. Since the human being is also a being of value, then studying the human being becomes not only a question of what the human being "is" but also what the human being is constantly becoming by virtue of the values he, she, or they manifest. This emanation makes the human being, and consequently human study, a fundamentally incomplete intellectual endeavor. It involves studying that which is always directed beyond the present.

Jaspers, whose remarks on authentic human reality serve as the epigraph to this reflection, took these dimensions of human study to heart in his philosophy of existence.[3] For Jaspers, as for Edmund Husserl, the realm of science proper is factual.[4] Because science is also concerned with repeatability, as a function of experimentation and prediction, science is concerned with laws, which are propositions whose formulations over the behavior of relevant phenomena have no exception. To have no exception means to cover the entire scope of a domain, which means that prediction works beyond the present to the future—in fact, for all time. Jaspers reminds us that the scientific perspective is not the entire story of reality because it is not the entire story of truth.[5] Truth, for Jaspers, has several manifestations. There is pragmatic truth, where a judgment either works or it does not. The cognition of this aspect of truth we share with the rest of living things, where extinction is the price of error. Something is either edible or it is not; it is safe to do some activities and dangerous to do others, and so forth. Then there is truth that comes from consciousness-in-general. This is the truth from which science and many social activities are born. This truth is not functionalist, as in pragmatic truth, but is instead guided by correctness. In Jaspers's words: "It proves itself by evidence."[6] From there, we move on to truth "at the level of *spirit*," which is governed by thought or ideas. But beyond this truth is the truth about the self, where we are critical and self-questioning, where we go through the existential experience and movement of standing out, of dealing with the implications of our not only being in the world but also being capable of evaluating how we live it. This move draws us to the realization of a reality greater than ourselves, what Jaspers calls the "Encompassing." This truth he calls *Existenz*. When we move beyond looking at laws of nature and questions of the self, when we begin to take on questions of reality in the grand sense, in the sense of Absolute reality, we face that which is infinitely bigger than our grandest aspirations and hopes. We face, that is, Reality Itself, and for that, we seek Truth but lack the mediating dynamics at the other levels. Our concepts are at best a leap since that Truth cannot be subordinated to any category—even, paradoxically, itself. We, therefore, here experience "truth in *faith*."[7] But since we share with this search the ever-transcending movement from completion, we face a paradox. *We* existentially transcend natural laws while Reality always transcends *us*, yet we are able to speak about that elusive, paradoxically transphenomenal phenomenon, which, paradoxically, transcends also phenomena. For Jaspers, this was possible through engagements with the symbolic, which he calls *cyphers*. "The cypher," he writes, "is neither object nor subject. It is objectivity which is permeated by subjectivity and in such a way that Being becomes present in the whole."[8] The "whole" is never completely ours. It stands as the mysterious in reality that reminds us of our limits. Thus, "The Symbol is *infinite*. In pursuing the symbol, and with it the experience of essential reality, thought stands still. No thought is adequate to the symbol. The symbol opens us up for Being and shows us all Being."[9] The symbolic, then, by virtue of being infinite, is the indeterminate revelation of reality. Its indeterminacy is its leitmotif of mystery.

One might wonder at this point what Jaspers means by "reality." Reality is all that transcends thought without loss. "Authentic reality is the being that *cannot be thought in terms of possibility*.... Where what I know is one of many possibilities, I am dealing with an appearance, not with reality itself. I can think about an object only if I think of it as a possibility. Reality is, therefore, what resists all thought."[10] And further: "A completely thinkable reality would not be reality any longer, but only an *addendum* to what is possible. It would not be an origin, and therefore the real thing, but something derivative and *secondary*. And indeed, we are overcome by a feeling of nothingness the moment we imagine that we have transformed all of reality into conceivability; that is to say that we have not put this total conceivability in the place of reality."[11]

The search for Truth is a philosophical one through which we encounter a struggle with religion as well. Religion, whose province is meaning, myth, and faith, has the luxury of taking on this task without the encumbrance of the limits faced by philosophy.[12] Its media can, therefore, be poetic, mythic, and mystical. Philosophy, after all, seems to stop where the mystical and the faithful would both leap, although, as Jaspers correctly points out, "Reason is 'mysticism for the understanding'" and that "Philosophy through the millennia is like one great hymn to reason—though it continually misunderstands itself as finished knowledge, and declines continually into reasonless understanding."[13] Thus, the study of the encounter with such leaps stands at the level of the symbolic. The symbolic, exemplified by the effort to understand that which simultaneously points to and away from that which signifies, points us to transcendence. It thus resists, at the categorial level, our efforts at its domestication. Writes Jaspers:

> The symbol is the complete presentness of Being. In it is the strongest, most penetrating mode of being present of whatever is. Essential reality is more, is inwardly more gripping, than the empirical reality which only dominates my daily life. If someone says, "God is more real than this table here," it is a distorted expression. In no way is God real like the table; it is a difference not of degree but of kind. Being bound by the absolutism of empirical existence closes one off from the essential reality of the Divinity. The assertion of God's existence as an existence greater than that of this table is a tyrannical form of the will to believe which, as a matter of fact, still clings to empirical reality as the absolute.[14]

The human being's ability to live and construct meaning at the level of consciousness, spirit, and faith stands as a limit to physical reductionism, what Jaspers means by empirical existence, and reveals a dimension of human reality manifested by the symbolic. Indeed, the human being *is* symbolic in the sense that the determinate features of human beings always stand as a "part" of human reality, which renders the human being an indeterminate feature, always, of a greater story.

Others Are More Than Symbolic

The symbolic is not solely a matter of struggles for mediations with Absolute reality. It is also part of the struggle for the glimpse of such transcendence in the experience of one's fellow human being. To understand this dimension of the symbolic, we could think through Edmund Husserl's struggle with the question of others in the Fifth Meditation of his *Cartesian Meditations*. There, Husserl turned to a peculiar problem of transcendental phenomenology. Phenomenology begins through a suspension of or orientation away from the natural attitude, the ordinary presumptions we have about the world. From there, there is the move to the realization of the intentional features of the objects of investigation. Now, there is a danger of rendering the objects of investigation in a naturalistic way, which would in effect be to throw them back into the natural attitude through an ontologizing of the phenomenological moment. To eliminate that, each step must be taken with recognition of suspension or parenthesizing or bracketing. Realization of the act of doing so carries with it a conscious apprehension of the objects of consciousness. Thus, at each stage, essential features are sought without essential*ism*. The movements through acts of free variation, where an ongoing thematic of the object is presented, exemplifies phenomenological work. Husserl is here interested in examining the question of phenomenology's rigor and its significance for philosophical work. Toward the first objective, he in effect moves—mathematician as he was—in the form of a syntactical demonstration of phenomenology's syntax. This he calls a phenomenology of phenomenology, or, less circular sounding, a metatheory of phenomenology, which leads him to questions, if pursued farther, that takes him into philosophical questions that exemplify phenomenological philosophy or what he calls transcendental phenomenology.[15] As Alfred Schutz describes this move, "Phenomenological philosophy deals with the activities of the transcendental ego, with the constitution of space and time, with the constitutions of intersubjectivity, with the problems of life and death, with the problems of monads; indeed, it is an approach to the questions hitherto called metaphysical."[16]

Transcendental phenomenology also includes the exploration of phenomenology through the relentless advancement of the phenomenological criterion of radicality. Phenomenology must be radical because of the suspension of the natural attitude, which means the suspension even of methodological security. If even the method is brought into question, then the paradox of a method of not presupposing a method follows. After going through a variety of phases of phenomenological work and having arrived at what he considers the grounding of phenomenology in the transcendental ego—the ego as understood at the level of the meaning of all meaning or the relationship constituted by the intelligibility of thought—Husserl then faces the problem of how meaning can function at the level of evidence and how evidence carries with it peculiarly social dimensions that raise the question of other intending subjects.

Here, in brief, is the problem that unfolds. How can one intend another consciousness when the natural attitude, which brings along with it the ontological features of the "object," is suspended? Why is this a problem? It is so for the mere fact that a human being is not like another object because a human being is ultimately an object only in part. An object can be apprehended solely as an object because of its place in the typicality of things. An instance of one thing, in other words, is no different *ontologically* (although debatable metaphysically) than any other instance of that thing, which means the transcending feature(s) of the object—its "being" so to speak—carries with it simply the nothingness that exemplifies any being without phenomena. It is this feature of things that make them "replaceable." They can literally stand in as instances of each other. For conscious beings, however, the features of consciousness they share with each other carry with them the features of a lived reality, and where that reality carries with it memory and values—along with hopes and dreams—that which constitutes *existence* (that is, standing out, standing apart) carries with it unique narratives that collapse them into singular identities *internal* to their being. To intend another human being, then, does not carry with it the typical features of external phenomena. The internal upsurge of the other human being brings with it the values and sufferings of that other human being and these are features that exemplify the paradox of a being whose natural condition is unnatural—in fact, whose being constitutes *the unnatural* or, as I prefer, *queer.*

The encounter with another human being is the prime condition of irreplaceability. No one else can be Harry or Mary, Jacques or Jean, Jasmine or Mohamed, Mpho or Tshepo. Phenomenology, thus, encounters something informative in the limits embodied by each human being—namely, open phenomena or, in transcendental phenomenological terms, reality. This limit is what Jaspers means when he refers to the irreplaceability of Existenz. Its irreplaceability means that it finds no conceptual substitute. Nothing can stand in for another human being, for that thing would simply be yet another human being instead of the one in question. Although it is tempting, using such metaphysical notions as the identity of indiscernibles, where two indiscernible objects may have a distinct identity—to claim the triviality of this point by appealing to its application to any two seemingly identical objects—the difference is that the purely conceptual level alone is insufficient for the human "object." The phenomenological turn, in other words, reveals the difference between human beings and other objects. There is no law that governs the content of what stands beneath such phenomena, for instead of a being whose difference is inconsequential, the richness of the human being beneath human phenomena or appearance is manifold. We know this not only from the discursive practices creatively constituted by each human being but also from the cues that come from each human being's gift of intimacy.

An example of such intimacy is love. Let me illustrate by way of experience. In my late twenties, I stood in a graveyard under the hot late-August summer sun subsumed by the grief of having just placed my best friend six feet under. I was overwhelmed by the sight of the many coffins in the hole where he was placed. He was Catholic and was buried in a Catholic cemetery that was unfortunately overcrowded, so there were several caskets with deceased people in each grave. The coffins suggested a level of anonymity that militated against the uniqueness of my friend. Not only was it clear that *his grave* would be a misnomer, but the many coffins hinted at the nihilistic dimensions of death; they reminded me of the many who have died, of the ongoing process of death, which means a return to nonliving things in the universe. There is something almost contradictory about nonliving *things*, for as things they continue to be. As I said, I was overwhelmed. Turning away, consumed by tears, I was approached by a woman who said to me, entirely missing the point, "Don't cry. You will have other friends."

The replaceability of other human beings has been a project of human communities from the moment people realized that they are also resources. Such a functionalist view of people renders them replaceable by virtue of *use*. Yes, one can always have other friends, if it is friends one wants. But mourning is not about other friends. It is about *this* friend, *this* person. The peculiarity of love is the conviction it brings forth. In love, we make a judgment both about the world and the beloved. That judgment is that the world is better with the existence of the beloved. The beloved, in other words, *ought* to exist. That judgment is the value of the beloved. As both valued and a source of value, the beloved is absolutely unique. His corpse is no doubt still there, establishing his being or once having been, but my friend no longer exists.

In love, the direction of value is other-directed. The baby in one's arms overflows with the elation of deserved existence through the intentional act of love. The realization of love, marked by the embrace, by the circle that constitutes a world of being, faces its opposite in the selfish consciousness of functionality. There, the direction is self-focused. The baby in one's arms is there *for* the parent, the beloved *for* the lover. Such relationships are replaceable by virtue of being primarily *roles*. A shift in the place of irreplaceability follows. Where the self is the point of attachment, then all others are replaceable. Where the self is regarded as insignificant or at least not primary, others are irreplaceable. The familiar themes of sadism and masochism find a place here. The former consciousness, solipsistic, has a world that revolves around it. The latter seeks a solid point around which to revolve. Beyond this dualism is the possibility of recognizing the value of both others' and one's irreplaceability through shared responsibility for replaceability. In other words, the constant possibility of a collapsed functionalism raises the responsibility for the value of irreplaceability. This value is compounded by the impact of the inevitability of death. Ali Shariati summarizes this beautifully:

> When we love someone in order to be loved, or when we are kind to someone so that we can receive a favor, we are businessmen. Love consists of giving up everything for the sake of a goal and asking nothing in return. This requires one to make a great choice. What is the choice? To choose oneself to die—or some other objective—so another can live and some ideals be realized.[17]

The theme of irreplaceability and its relation to death has been a source of classical myth. In ancient Kmt, Isis attempts to regain her dismembered husband Osiris by planting his heart—in other versions his penis—in a tree by the bank of a river through which Horus is born. In other versions, she reanimates Osiris, copulates with him, after which he goes to the underworld, and she carries on pregnant with their child. Horus is the replacement for Osiris, but in truth, he is and *is not* Osiris. In Sumer, Gilgamesh seeks his lost soul mate Enkidu, whose longing to return to his "wild man" state was never realized except as the gift, ironically through a curse, of death. And among the Hellenes, there is the story of Orpheus and Eurydice, where Orpheus' love takes him into the Netherworld to regain his beloved only to lose her through the temptation, through a lack of faith in her voice, to look back at her during his doomed ascent. The Orphic myth also offers a special theme of music and sound. Orpheus, a musician with the sweetest voice, sings and plays the lyre so beautifully that it stimulates the most restful sleep (another instance of death's embrace) for which he receives the consent of Hades, the god of the Netherworld, to leave with his beloved, but Hades warns him to trust his ears instead of his eyes. "The cypher," writes Jaspers, "is listened to, not cognized."[18] The story behind these myths is striking. One never regains whom one has lost. A new version surfaces, with the same function, but it is not what one ultimately seeks, which is a form of return. In the Orphic version, the second loss, begun by sound, which is always distant, leads to Orpheus' dismemberment at the hands of a group of Ciconian Maenads. "Dismembering" reveals the limits of "remembering."

Remembering is, of course, memory. Memory is a continuation of that which is irreplaceable. Perhaps the most striking exemplar of this is the process of naming. When named, a thing is transformed into a schema and thereby becomes a "member." A pet, for example, is an animal that was part of a cycle interrupted by a process of being pulled out by virtue of being named and thereby brought into the sphere of the unique. When it dies (that is, is dismembered), the pet recedes into the sphere of memory. When we think of ourselves, those whom we remember are realized as having been part of our whole; they live on with and in us as phantom limbs and organs, present by virtue of their absence.

Others Beyond "Man"

There is another implication of the phenomenological problem of others, which can also be called the problem of intersubjectivity. Irreplaceability is not, as we have seen, a natural condition. By that, I mean that it is not properly speaking a feature of reality beyond consciousness. Properly speaking nothing in nature "replaces" anything else. Each thing simply is *qua* what it is only once. It is in a thematized world, a world conditioned by meaning, that replaceability can emerge. What this means, then, is that both replaceability and irreplaceability are functions of a world constituted by consciousness. The problem in Husserl's Fifth Meditation, thus, returns as the problem of the grounding of the social world by which both the meaningful and the unique can come about. We see here, then, a transcendental argument. A necessary condition for irreplaceability is replaceable things. But why are some things replaceable and other things not?

There is the replaceable in the sense that one has another whose presence makes the former's absence inconsequential. Presence and absence are parts of schemas of use. So, the replaceable depends on a system in which something functions as part of a whole. Difficulty surfaces here when the whole faces its demise. How does one replace something that functions as whole? The problem is further exacerbated by the conditions that constitute something as whole, for, we may then ask if the part must be constituted by its intended features toward something greater than itself, what can we make of a rejection of going farther? What do we make of parts that begin to function as a whole?

At the heart of all notions of irreplaceability is the rejection of functionality. The irreplaceable object becomes, that is, an end-value in itself. It is, in other words, deontological. It must be.

At this point, we face what existentialists call "seriousness." This attitude is one through which we flip the cart of values in front of the proverbial horse by concealing our role in their creation. We forget, in other words, that it is "we," intersubjectively understood, who bring values to the world, and consequently their change, and even their elimination depends on "us." In seriousness, we "naturalize" our values, rendering them material features of the world. We should here be reminded of Michel Foucault's remarks on the unfolding significance of language in *Les mots et les choses* ("Words and Things").[19] The ascent of language becomes, he argues, like proverbial fire gone out of control, consuming everything, wherein it's new, rising forms, new discourses, may render obsolete the *discourse* of man. We may now ask about what is at stake in man's discursive replaceability? As Sylvia Wynter queried, how do we theorize the *human* after man?[20]

We here return to the initial problem of the human study of the human being. The elimination or transcending of man for the sake of the human raises the question of what rises beyond the "whole." The search for the human cannot be a replacement of "man," for it would be a return, but it must instead be a leap that is paradoxically a limit. After all, to leap beyond the human, beyond the openness that is also the world—indeed, the only world—in which and through which we inhabit and constitute such possibilities renders our own irreplaceability, transcendentally, because "we" cannot replace ourselves. The underside of the human, in other words, is the human *for* the human, the human in the face of the symbolic.

A feature of the present is that we confuse the cyclical patterns of societal ascent and decay to suggest a permanence of our species. Our estimated 220,000-year march into significance is marked by an unnerving sense of crying out into the cosmos only to hear our own echo. We allow many other species to fall sway to the consequences of our folly to a point of naivety as we seem to forget that none of these species will ever inhabit the earth again. The implications of a healthy understanding of and respect for irreplaceable dimensions of ourselves and their symbiotic relation to our fellow human beings and fellow living creatures call for a radical transformation of the values by which we have been living. Such a turn would make all the difference between respect and the sacred on the one hand and contempt for all things living on the other. I wrote of myths earlier. Among our many myths are those that look at the human condition as standing between fire (the sun) and those points so far from it that they are the epitome of things cold and lifeless. The cold and lifeless is a frozen reality, a reality that will not move from itself but remains locked in its ossified contempt for all beings in whose heart beats a healthy respect for things greater than themselves. There is an irony here, for the irreplaceable, instead of signifying closure, instead of signifying being frozen, becomes that which must be treasured and which we must learn to go beyond by placing it into its proper place of memory. "Man," however, as Alain Locke reminds us, "does not, cannot, live in a valueless world."[21] The question, thus, rises of the kinds of values by which we live our lives. Replaceable values, along with replaceable people and things, provide the illusion of a ceaseless life.[22] It trivializes things in an economy of a continued same.

I close, then, with a thought, reminiscent of Osiris and Orpheus, on the jazz musician's performance. Jazz performance beyond swing is often irritatingly boring on film. It stands as something that is irreplaceably live and at its best when lighting is punctuated by layers of darkness to achieve a dreamlike atmosphere that tempts us to focus less on what we are looking at and appreciate its grandeur in the world of sound. Perhaps this is a reminder to us that there are some things that, when we see them beckoning us, we must also remember to listen to as we ascend to the future that we alone can live.

Notes

1. Karl Jaspers, *Reason and Existenz: Five Lectures*, trans. William Earle (New York, NY: Noonday, 1955), 62.
2. Peter Caws, *Ethics from Experience* (Boston, MA: Jones and Bartlett Publishers, 1996), 82.
3. Jaspers's main ideas emerge in his three-volume work *Philosophie* (Berlin, Germany: J. Springer-Verlag, 1932). I have chosen to cite from the shorter volumes since his subsequent formulations are more succinct and those texts are more easily acquired. Most of my discussion pertains to volumes 2 and 3 of his great work.
4. Jaspers's views will unfold in the course of this discussion. For Husserl's critique of the relativism of facts, see "Philosophie als strenge Wissenschaft," *Logos* I (1910–1911): 289–341; "Philosophy as Rigorous Science," in *Phenomenology and the Crisis of Philosophy: Philosophy as Rigorous Science and Philosophy and the Crisis of European Man*, Trans. and Intro. Quentin Lauer (New York, NY: Harper & Row, 1965), 71–147.
5. Jaspers's criticisms of scientism is that it fails to account for crucial elements of science, which are (1) that it is particular, (2) that it can provide no goals for life, and (3) that it cannot ground itself or provide its meaning on its own terms. See his *Philosophy of Existence*, 10. These criticisms, by the way, do not exemplify a rejection of science but instead state its limits. For Jaspers, science, for example, offers philosophy a sense of its own limits. Philosophy should not, in other words, confuse itself with the exactitude of scientific knowledge (10–11).
6. *Philosophy of Existence*, 39.

7. *Philosophy of Existence*, 39.
8. Karl Jaspers, *Truth and Symbol*, trans. Jean T. Wilde, William Kluback, and William Kimmel (Albany, NY: New College and University Press, Inc., 1959), 35.
9. *Truth and Existence*, 40.
10. *Philosophy of Existence*, 69.
11. *Philosophy of Existence*, 70.
12. For a similar view, see Keiji Nishitani, *Religion and Nothingness*, trans. Jan Van Bragt (Berkeley, CA: University of California Press, 1982).
13. *Philosophy of Existence*, 60.
14. *Truth and Symbol*, 41.
15. I would like to thank my colleague Kenneth Knies at Sacred Heart University for remarks that led to my reformulation of this and the succeeding paragraph.
16. Alfred Schutz, "Some Leading Concepts of Phenomenology," in *The Collected Papers, Volume 1, The Problem of Social Reality*, ed. Maurice Natanson (The Hague, The Netherlands: Martinus Nijhoff, 1962), 115–116.
17. Ali Shariati, *Man and Islam*, trans. Fatolla Marjani (North Haledon, NJ: Islamic Publication International, 1981), 61–62.
18. *Truth and Symbol*, 41.
19. Michel Foucault, *Les mots et les choses: Une Archeologie des Sciences Humaines* (Paris, France: Gallimard, 1966), especially 398. Available in English through Vintage as *The Order of Things: An Archaeology of the Human Sciences*, trans. Alan Sheridan (New York: Vintage, 1994).
20. This is the question of her keynote in the Institute for Caribbean Thought seminar in her honor entitled, "The Human After Man: A Seminar in Honor of Sylvia Wynter," at the University of the West Indies at Mona, Jamaica (June 2002), which led to B. Anthon Bogues (ed.), *After Man, Towards the Human: Critical Essays on the Thought of Sylvia Wynter* (Kingston, JA: Ian Randle, 2006). Her thoughts on this question emerge in several essays such as "The Ceremony Must Be Found: After Humanism," *boundary 2* XII–XIII, nos. 1–2 (Spring/Fall 1984): 19–71; "Is 'Development' a Purely Empirical Concept or also 'Teleological'?" A Perspective from 'We the Underdeveloped,'" in Aguibou Y. Yansané (ed.), *Prospects for Recovery and Sustainable Development in Africa* (Westport, CT: Greenwood Press, 1996), 299–316; "Towards the Sociogenic Principle: Fanon, Identity, the Puzzle of Conscious Experience, and What It is Like to Be a 'Black,'" in Mercedes F. Durán-Cogan and Antonio Gómez-Moriana (eds.), *National Identities and Socio-Political Changes in Latin America* (New York, NY: Routledge, 2001), 30–66.
21. Alain Locke, *The Philosophy of Alain Locke: Harlem Renaissance and Beyond*, Leonard Harris (ed.) (Philadelphia, PA: Temple University Press, 1989), 34.
22. Two examples of replaceability at the level of groups and at the level of the individual are contemporary slavery and cosmetic surgery. Contemporary slavery is on the rise because it is more profitable than past slavery. Why is it so profitable? Because overpopulation has cheapened the value of human beings, so slaves are now cheaper, and mechanisms of war and political conflicts cultivate precariousness of life and accompanying vulnerabilities. With regard to cosmetic surgery, the ambiguity of replaceability comes to the fore since replacement here is also augmentation. For discussion of contemporary slavery, see Kevin Bales, *Disposable People: New Slavery in the Global Economy* (Berkeley, CA: University of California Press, 1999) and Jane Anna Gordon, *Statelessness and Contemporary Enslavement* (New York, NY: Routledge, 2020). For discussion of surgery, wherein the parts of the individual affect her or his other sense of being whole, see Sander L. Gilman, *Creating Beauty to Cure the Soul: Race and Psychology in the Shaping of Aesthetic Surgery* (Durham, NC: Duke University Press, 1998).

Chapter 8

Disaster, Ruin, and Permanent Catastrophe

The inevitability of permanent catastrophe haunts human existence. Despite the efforts of our parents, our parents' parents, and theirs through to remote ancestors, each of us lives with the realization that we came out of nothing and will one day, if not return, succumb to what for many is a foreboding nothing. I come to this question of permanent catastrophe from my work in existential phenomenology, especially its African diasporic or Africana instantiation. An important element of existential philosophy is the primacy it gives to contingency. The human world is governed by the reality of that which could be otherwise. As a consequence, that which does not occur by accident is often simultaneously that which is not necessary. This leads to an additional view, that the notion of human nature should be abandoned in favor of a human condition. Essence, in other words, is that which is brought *into* the human world instead of being that which governs it. As a form of phenomenology, this approach raises the question of how one examines phenomena once one has bracketed, parenthesized, or, as I prefer, suspended one's naïve ontological commitments and presuppositions. Such an act offers the unusual distinction of being able to articulate essence without essentialism. The first is a description while the latter is a prescription, a claim about what ought to be the way things are beyond the description. As a form of Africana philosophy, the descriptions that follow from this approach take into account a set of imperatives raised by the historical emergence of African diasporic peoples— namely, that something has happened in the Euromodern world with regard to what it means to be human, to be free, and to engage in justificatory practices. The result is to take seriously the human condition under the lived reality of the organizational practices that created such shifts, and these include colonialism and racism.

A catastrophe is something that occurs, which means there is a precatastrophic condition. So, the question is raised, Why, then, as something that comes into being catastrophe is not also what could go out of it? There is a peculiar symmetry implicit in this question; a changing world needs continued change for balance. But what if change is asymmetrical? What if there were some things that simply come into being and others that just go, permanently, out of being? What if, in other words, there is a genuine end? We know there is such at least implicitly in ideas about the universe or, if we will, pluriverse, that, for example, from a quantum of reality there was a cooling of energy expanding into our physical reality and it will all eventually end—at least as we understand it.[1]

In a mundane sense, the eventual end of all there is haunts everyone's existence, but it does not do so for those of us who expect our own death to precede such events, which means it is a concern more for posterity or for those of us who hope to be remembered by such. A viable sense of permanent catastrophe requires, then, more modest concerns, in spite of the apocalyptic elements of the phrase. Given our specific history at the writing of this reflection, it behooves us to consider, at least, perspectives from which the world, in a word, ended, through which to understand permanent catastrophe in what ultimately may make more sense to us—that is, in ultimately human terms.

Wherein We Live

To say a permanent catastrophe is devastating in human terms would be an understatement. Immediate annihilation would leave nothing for reflection. Thus, realization of the event as such requires survivors or, from the perspective of the present, an imagined one who, comprehending its significance, laments the loss. Reflecting in such terms calls for an understanding of that plague on the human spirit and our efforts at its alleviation—namely, misery.

Sigmund Freud, in *Das Unbehagen in der Kultur* ("Unease in Culture"), popularly known in English under the title of *Civilization and Its Discontents*, examines three sources of human misery. They are nature, our bodies, and other people. The first holds the terror and contingency of natural events such as being struck down by lightning or being swallowed up by a cyclone. The second is physically from within, as our genes, our physical frailty, and the reality of simply being mortal remind us. The third is the social world, in which constraints are placed in a dialectical tension with desire, wants, and social well-being. Unable to control others as one could a tool, and for others facing a similar problem regarding the self, the human world becomes, in Freud's Hobbesian model of life, brutish and short, a world of conflict in which individuals are subordinated at times by force but often by other means such as the stultifying weight of guilt. Yet guilt could only make sense where there is a sense of a deeply rooted good, and as this social world is one in which the challenges of nature and the limitations of our bodies could be, if not overcome, at least placed into some relief through the substitution of a human world, one in which the human being is at home, the effect of culture is, as Freud observed in its projection, almost isomorphically placed onto reality itself as a prosthetic god.

My aim here is not psychoanalytical so much as to affirm a shared observation of all humanists—that the humanity of all human beings requires, tautologically as it is, a human world imbued with human reality. This world is marked by a fundamental feature that bothered positivist adherents of inquiry, including Freud, and continues the same for their intellectual descendants who would prefer a neat reality of well-measured and precise phenomena. The lived-reality of meaning does not behave as such. This aspect poses problems in one sense because of its fecundity. Where precision, a necessary element of scientific inquiry, is demanded, assertions of extension dominate over those of what philosophers of language call "intension." Abstract as this may be, it amounts to this: an extensional language has no gap between what is asserted and what is so in reality. It is in a one-to-one relation with what, where Being serves as the model, proverbially there is, which leaves no room for error. An intensional language is not in a one-to-one relation, which means an assertion could have other possibilities. The first would like to reduce the world to signs that simply point to "things." The second addresses signs that point beyond signs and things. It is, in the language of Ernst Cassirer, "symbolic."[2] In his philosophy of culture, Cassirer reminds us that this synthetic term, whose etymology refers to throwing things together, is the basis of the peculiarly human world. It is a world lived through symbols and their forms, a world, in other words, of meaning.

Thus, for the human being, from this point of view, to lose culture, to be barred from it, to not enter it, to be outside of the framework through which it is made manifest, is to suffer disintegration, destruction, and ruin.

Failing to enter culture is something otherwise. It is, as Jean-Jacques Rousseau reflected in his *Discourses*, to be an animal, and a fairly intelligent one, but not a human being beyond the biological constellation of organic makeup. One could behave as such in a world of signs, as do so many other animals such as cats and dogs, but the vast constellation of meanings that make up the human world would not be on the horizon, for even "horizon" would, under conditions limited to signification instead of symbols, not make any sense. Culture, in this view, is, thus, a transcendental condition of a genuinely human reality.

Talk, then, of cultureless human beings is nonsense. This is because culture, in the radicalized philosophical sense, is constitutive of human reality—or at least any reality that would be meaningful for a human being. Within this framework, there are organizations of meanings into what have been commonly called "folkways" and "mores." These elements, while features of culture, are not the sole determinants of it. Thus, it is fallacious to ascribe the absence of culture on the bases of differences along these lines. Folkways and mores may differ, but they stand, in the end, as manifestations of the same human condition and phenomenon.[3]

Yet it is coherent to talk about "a" culture as simply the expression of culture in ways that form the identity or fusion of a people. This is because individuals could meet under shared, meaningful conditions. This meeting could transcend the singularity of a chance encounter and become over time the formation of a community. This fusion, so to speak, is conditioned by what existentialists call the lived reality of projects. Where meaning is exhausted, the consequence is decay.

Wherein We Die—of Catastrophe, Disaster, and Monstrosity

Decay, as we know, continues past death, but it does not always have to. Sometimes, only a part of us dies and begins a process through which our impending death is paradoxically lived. This process offers symptoms through which its story could be told. Decadence, as Nietzsche showed, is a process of dying whose social symptom is nihilism.[4] He meant by this the emergence of antivalue as an expression of value. The latter, properly understood, is a living affirmation of life. The former pushes life to the side in an almost automated and dissociated performance of rules under the guise of "morals."[5] What is crucial about lived-values is that they involve active participation in the production of meaning, which brings to the fore the question of responsibility for what is produced. This classic existential model raises the question of meaning in life through which emerges also the meaning *of* life.

Jane Anna Gordon and I reflected on some of the consequences of this portrait of culture in our book *Of Divine Warning: Reading Disaster in the Modern Age.*[6] The title, while an accurate portrayal of our thesis and argument, turned out to be misleading since some readers took "divine" and "warning" to mean some kind of eschatological, prophetic religious treatise. What we meant was this: while disasters are discussed all across the globe, the question of the *meaning* of disaster receives scant attention. The matter becomes complicated once we locate the category of thought into which such reflection belongs. To call an event a disaster, after all, is a judgment about a circumstance. The earth, too many forget, is a physical entity caught in the gravitational field of the sun, and as it relates to the gravity of other entities and its own internal physical structure, such things as volcanic eruptions, tidal waves, and climate change are part of the course. Whether life exists or not on the planet, the earth will continue to spin on its axis and revolve around the sun until the latter swells, incinerates it, and, if the conditions are right, much in this area of our galaxy collapses under the weight of its implosion, provided, of course, the remote chance of asteroid 2013TV135 colliding with our planet in 2032 does not prove our demise otherwise.[7] All this is a different story when life takes a form that asks: What would all this *mean*?

For one thing, it would mean, should that life aspire to persist, a catastrophe. From the Greek *katastrephein*, the term literally means to fall down and come to an end. As we are not born standing, we experience catastrophe as falling back, which raises the question: Can we continue to rise again and again? Falling is a mythic phenomenon in the sense of raising the question of meaning beyond its initial appearance. That meaning beyond signification makes the study of this phenomenon in the realm of the human sciences, where even the meaning of meaning receives scrutiny. The concept of disaster fits into this model well, since, as its etymology reveals—from the Italian *dis astro*, transformed through Latin from the Greek *astron*, which amounts to "fallen star or planet"—it is about that which literally falls from the sky, which we might as well call the heavens. And since falling from heaven is not a good thing, the additional question becomes whether the fallen object has come to its end. A problem arises when witnessing such an event is encounter with something portentous, which is why we often ask, upon seeing it, "What does it mean?" This question marks the event as a possible beginning.

Now, of course, if the fallen star's message is for the witness, then the event stops there. But if it is not, if it moves through the witness, then the sign, so to speak, continues. That means the event of "falling" is transformed into a series, which Jane Anna Gordon and I call "the sign continuum." What is striking about this continuation is that the witness is caught up into the sign and becomes, in effect, also a sign, and if it is a sign of becoming a sign for others, she, he, or they become a warning. As the origins are from the heavens, a location associated with divinity, this warning has the mythic quality of a divine warning.

A divine warning in Latin is issued in the word *monstrum*, which, in the infinitive is *monere* (to warn), from which we get, in English, "monster." Words such as "demonstrate," "remonstrate," "admonish," and "admonition," relate to this unusual phenomenon at the heart of which is a disaster. The question in the face of monsters (and monstrosities), then, is: what do they mean? What are they telling us? If we think through the mythic structure of a message from the heavens, of what monsters signify, they mean, in a nutshell, that "we" (that is, whomever the sign is for) are doing something wrong or that there is something we are supposed to be doing to prevent the production of monsters. In effect, a disaster is a call for intervention, for action. The error, then, is to focus on the monster instead of what stimulated its appearance.

An acute instance of this in recent times is the COVID-19 disease brought on by infection from the novel coronavirus SARS-CoV-2. Despite illustrations of the virus, the fact of the matter is that no one actually "sees" it coming; its invisibility makes its appearance a sign at first in those whose symptoms of the disease are embodied and then through the vast array of signs to prevent its transmission among those who are asymptomatic carriers of the virus. Being both present when symptomatically evident and when absent, the virus is terrifyingly everywhere. It, thus, transformed at first the symptomatically afflicted into sign continua to be avoided, since transmission, continuation, is the way of such signs, but the virus' ubiquity produced a profound assault on the sociality of all human beings who must be kept at a physical distance from each other at all cost. Life under COVID-19 makes, or perhaps reminds us, humanity a disaster.

Returning to our initial Freudian triumvirate of nature, our bodies, and each other, the course of catastrophe, disaster, and monstrosity offer corrective possibilities in terms of natural science and technology for the first, medical science and health regimens for the second, and social psychology and good governing for the last. But these are each a technocratic response that elides its deeper meaning, especially in terms of the last two. Responding to our limitations through corrections of the form of healthy behavior and systems of rules organizing those behaviors work the extent to which they are meaningful. What, however, if meaning itself suffers the catastrophe? What kind of disaster would that be? What are its monsters?

Once Whole, Left in Ruin

We come now to the focus of these reflections. In the words of Robert Ginsberg: "Humanity is the greatest ruin. Mythology and theology, philosophy's handmaids, identify us as fallen. The Golden Age preceded our history. It is the happy state we left behind."[8]

This happy state—which we saw earlier is the infantile cry of conservatism—is a presumed one, since we think of it as such only as a projection onto it. How can we, after all, remember a time of happiness when the conditions of its meaning—indeed, its even being meaningful—were absent? Would we not need evidence, a "mark," as it were? This, amusingly, is one of the concerns Freud had about circumcision; the "memory" of the event is in the evidence of absent foreskin.[9] Men with their foreskin represent a former wholeness that those without now lack. The situation of course becomes more complicated with women since it could only work in a framework of bionormality in which the male body becomes *the* human body. Under that circumstance, the notion of lack in the lives of women becomes that of in effect never really being born. The matter is worsened for women as a form of "in the making" with the expectation of failed achievement—unless, of course, the subordination of this mythic meeting is achieved through technology, as we now see with the place of hormonal treatment, genetics, and surgery. The folly of the matter is evident in the subversion of wholeness through, as in Judaism, ethical wholeness, where the commanded absent foreskin becomes the inauguration of ethical life. This led, as we see in many countries today, to the normalization of circumcision to the point of making the uncircumcised the exemplification of lack. Such is the way of culture. For our purposes, the issue at hand is the presumption of prior happiness, even where the initial moment could have been premised on pain or mutilation. What, in other words, could make that prior state one of happiness?

If the presumption is that of no prior suffering, of the absence of suffering, as the model of happiness, then Nietzsche's counsel is a wise one; the best course is preemption—that is, never to have been born.[10] If that is the standard, then to be born is a disaster. It is to fall from the already fallen—to be a sign continuum—a catastrophe in which one is left ruined.

"Catastrophe" and "ruin" are intimately linked. The etymology of "ruin" is the Latin word *ruina*, which means to collapse or tumble down. For the curious, the ancient East African language Mdw Ntr offers a similar portrait, where there is a connection between *wAsi* (to be ruined) and *wA* (to fall into a condition). We are already here witnessing a structure of sign continua, where ancient Mdw Ntr and Greek words for falling to an end connect later on to a Latin word for falling down and then we move on to another Latin term, for "collapse" is from *collapsus*, which is the past participle of *collabi*, which literally means to fall together. The connection to *collaboration* is evident. This movement suggests a strong series of relations that many of us may wish to avoid—namely that embedded in our neighbor's catastrophe is our own.

A disaster, a fall from the heavens and its inaugurated sign continuum, always occurs somewhere at some time. A convergence of space and time in such a fall is a "disaster area." Such a place is in ruins. Somewhere, once teeming with life, at some point fell to the wayside, commencing a process of decay, perhaps from destruction, leading to the petrification of past hopes. The earth is littered with remains, historical in some cases, passing the eyes of most of us in others, many of which revealed a good fight against nature. Evidence abounds. Once lush fields turned desert. Ancient civilizations held out for as long as they could, because, after all, they thought they had forever, but at some point, there were the eventual final steps, the last closed door, the last precious artifact taken, the final look (poetically offering the risk, as the Book of Genesis attests, of turning us into salt), a lamented memory, as the final dwellers moved on.

One emigrates to live, but as Jean-Paul Sartre reflected on exhaustion in *Being and Nothingness*, the point at which one abandons a project is not always due to an externally imposed necessity.[11] "I cannot go on!" is often cried when one could, after all, take at least one more step. There is a point at which inhabitants abandon the project of the place, the point at which "here" becomes the place at which one can no longer live, the place at which the expectations for the self can no longer be realized. In other instances, the moment is cataclysmic. Death and destruction, as suffered by a village or city on a volcanic site, are instantaneous. In others, agents of destruction come in the form of human reapers of death, pillaging, and razing communities to the ground, decimating their infrastructure, with the rapidity of divine furies. And then there are plagues—infestations and disease eating away at life, spreading through the halls, infecting even the sociality of human life through the poisoning of proximity, rendering deadly the pleasure of touch and the warmth of breath. Such disasters at first leave a haunted presence of life in the wake of the flight taken by the uninfected, but in time, as abandoned homes, neglected streets, whole infrastructures, left to the ravages of bacteria, dust, and wind, decay, the ruined remains no longer stand as a site of sudden flight but instead as an above ground necropolis, indistinguishable from many other dead places beneath dirt, dust, sand, or the cold, barely livable, oxygen-deprive deepest depths of the sea.

Hubristic Hopes of Eternal Cities and Valuable Values

The marriage of science, technology, and language in the projected world of culture offers a seductive message of divine resistance. It enables human beings to forget we are not gods. If the city or empire could become eternal, so, we convince ourselves, we could achieve immortality. The existential term for this is "the spirit of seriousness."[12] It refers to a form of bad faith, lying to the self, in which we convince ourselves of a pleasing falsehood (in this case, our eternity or immortality) in an attempt to evade a displeasing truth (our mortality). The spirit of seriousness is an attitude in which values are materialized as devoid of human agency. This attitude tends to have a reflexive element, where the externality of the values, their objective credence, supposedly absolves responsibility for them. This view fails on two counts. Even if our values were objective, that does not absolve our responsibility for them since we ultimately must choose to adhere to them or not. In effect, the responsibility is also reflexively *for responsibility*. This ultimately makes their objective status irrelevant. But let us suppose they are objective and relevantly so. The question of why they are so, of their status *as values*, comes into play. Seriousness would, then, make our relation to such values irrelevant. But then, placed out of relations, the effect becomes our own irrelevance. Human presence or not, the values would live on. Placed in the framework of culture, the problem returns of human relations to human institutions. Without human beings, such institutions lose their animus. They become mere artifacts. Values, human institutions, in other words *live* as manifestations of human relations. We return to the human paradox: not to be ruined means to be a god. But that means not to be human. So the human being becomes, as Sartre famously put it, a "useless passion"—namely, the desire to be a god with aspirations and realizations that could only have come from not being one.

All this is, however, on an abstract level. Concretely, we are haunted by this realization each day. I recall my youngest child's response to looking at pictures taken of our family before he was born. He was perplexed. "Where," he asked, "am I?"

The answer, though true and logical, was nevertheless disturbing. "You did not yet exist."

The child's apprehension is honest. How could my youngest see as the family's good times any period in which he did not exist? How could we be, in such pictures, by virtue of our smiles, *happy*?

His consternation was an expression of our condition. We know there was a time when none of us existed. So even as we press on, as we struggle for some sense of permanence, the other side of the equation haunts us as well. There will be a time when we no longer exist. And even more radically, there could be the paradox of a time, as theoretical physicists argue, when there is no longer time.

Our passion is made concrete in our material objects and also in the variability of those relations the Germans call *Geist*, that is, (roughly) "spirit." Let us turn to examining the meaning of material objects.

A ruin is a peculiarly human phenomenon. It is the physical remains of a human project that has ceased. Our planet is littered with ruins. Gravestones, markers for the dead, also decay. They stick around although they no longer belong. Fossils, strewn about, portend our future. The earth moves on, and gravestones—representatives of solidity and stability—eventually slant, chip, topple over, or rot beneath a bed of weeds as they sink, slowly and assuredly into the fate of the fossil. Buildings go through decay and eventually fall into ruin. Across our planet, large-scale efforts for humanity to triumph over the forces of nature—"eternal cities" as some have been called—lie in ruin. They depend on the proverbial kindness of strangers to take pity on them, even in the form of maintaining them as ruins. Think of the ancient Roman city of Pompeii. Once vibrant, it reputedly became a necropolis within a day. Ginsberg defines ruin as "the irreparable remains of human construction that, by a destructive act or process, no longer dwells in the unity of the original, but may have its own unities that we can enjoy."[13] In ruins, time has come to a halt while paradoxically moving on. The ruined is temporally abandoned. "Pompeii," Ginsberg observes, "has ruined time. Its walls are timeless wells. We dip into their absoluteness of being, beyond categories of time and purpose. The innate brickness of the bricks has all the time in the world to educate our sensibility to it. Roman civilization recedes in consciousness, as we give ourselves over fully to this civilization of bricks."[14] What Ginsberg is getting at here transcends the facts of the materials scattered at a disaster area and left in ruin. He is pointing to, in his reference to "civilization," the living community that once animated them with meaning. Culture, and the societies in which it is made manifest, requires human beings for its continuation; it is, then, an expression of human beings in the peculiar recognition of the same dynamic of being born from another while being responsible for itself and producing others. This dimension of human existence shared by its macro-societal correlate is its fundamental incompleteness. As with a human life, where there is birth, maturation, decline, and death, there is a cyclical dynamic in societies, where, in the fervor of youth, they live as though they will do so forever. Whether the Temple of Karnak in Egypt, the Coliseum in Rome, the Parthenon in Athens, Inca Pyramids across Peru, or Aztec ones in Mexico, these ruins remind us of civilizations that once expected to last forever. They are testaments to the inevitable decay of all empires, cities, towns, villages, and homes. None of these lasts forever because no one lives forever, and even where such expectations are hoped for through memory, even the latter depends on the longevity of others. We are not, in ourselves, the children by whom we are remembered. At some point, there will be none.

Existentialists echoing Jean-Jacques Rousseau, such as Jean-Paul Sartre and Albert Camus, have written of the human being as a figure condemned to freedom. Although this freedom is a manifestation of our responsibility for how we live, it is also an understanding of our incompleteness. Each human being faces her or his self and correlative communities as a bastion of possibilities, but in each lived moment, many possibilities are dried up and potential shrinks to the point of reflection on a narrative, if one is afforded such a luxury, of what could have been and what might still be possible. The message in life, Ginsberg argues, channeling Arthur Schopenhauer, is not happiness

but for us to make ourselves ready when it is our time to die, which, paradoxically, is happiness because of having lived a life worth living. To achieve
one's goals in life, to have done what one sets out to do, transforms the threat
of death. The odd rationalization of not having done X or Y no longer holds
force. It is strange reasoning, since it presumes death has priorities. In the
second volume of *The World as Will and Representation*, Schopenhauer writes:

> There is only one inborn error [in humankind] and that is the notion that
> we exist in order to be happy.... We are nothing more than the will-to-
> live, and the successive satisfaction of all our willing is what we think
> of through the concept of happiness. So long as we persist in this inborn
> error, ... the world seems to us full of contradictions.... We may still try
> to put the blame for our individual unhappiness now on the circum-
> stances, now on other people, now on our own bad luck or even lack of
> skill, and we may know quite well how all these have worked together to
> bring it about, but this in no way alters the result that we have missed the
> real purpose of life, which, in fact, consists in being happy. The consid-
> eration of this then often proves to be very depressing, especially when
> life is already drawing to an end; hence, the countenances of almost all
> elderly persons wear the expression of what is called *disappointment*....
> Pains and sorrows, ... prove very real, and often exceed all expectations.
> Thus, everything in life is certainly calculated to bring us back from that
> original error and to convince us that the purpose of our existence is not
> to be happy.[15]

Schopenhauer draws the argument to its conclusion in a meditation on death:

> Dying is certainly to be regarded as the real aim of life; at the moment of
> dying, everything is decided which through the whole course of life was
> only prepared and introduced. Death is the result, the *résumé*, of life, or
> the total sum expression at one stroke [of] all the instruction given by life
> in detail and piecemeal, namely that the whole striving, the phenomenon
> of which is life, was a vain, fruitless, and self-contradictory effort, to have
> returned from which is a deliverance. Just as the whole slow vegetation
> of the plant is related to the fruit that at one stroke achieves a hundred-
> fold what the plant achieved gradually and piecemeal, so is life with its
> obstacles, deluded hopes, frustrated plans, and constant suffering related
> to death, which at one stroke destroys all, all that the person has willed
> and, thus, crowns the instruction given him by life.[16]

Ginsberg probably had passages like Schopenhauer's in mind when he
declared: "To philosophize is to ruin the human being."[17] Living a life worth
living is, after all, no easy task. This was ironically something of which
ancients were aware. Socrates' lover Alcibiades, for instance, described the

great philosopher and his practice in Plato's *Symposium* as "intoxicating," a form of poison, which Jacques Derrida rightly reminds us is a *phármako*, despite its medicinal effects.[18] Philosophy does not happen without a change from one state to another, without transformation, which means, as well, a form of gain through loss, especially where what are lost are our naivety and innocence. Some philosophers respond to this realization with sensible admission of its being what it is, while others are troubled by this phenomenon and attempt to overcome it. They attempt to lose the loss. Ginsberg prefers Schopenhauer's counsel: "We are the species living under the death sentence ... that it has passed against itself."[19] And he adds the existential situation of humanity in the 21st century: "The one constant truth for all humanity has been that we are each going to die. What differentiates the present generation from our predecessors is that we also bear the cross of destroying the species. If such a thing as sin exists, this is it. Killing a god might be forgiven by humanity, but we cannot forgive killing humanity."[20]

Powerful as Schopenhauer's and Ginsberg's words are, they reveal an underlying materiality of death through which there is a tendency, as embodied in empires and Euromodern thought, to take ourselves too seriously. Recall our initial observation on the spirit of seriousness. Many existentialists, from South through North, West through East, religious through to secular, agree on the dangers of too much self-investment. From Simone Weil to Keiji Nishitani, the counsel is what Weil calls "decreation"—emptying ourselves of egotistic attachment or, to make it plain, to not take ourselves too seriously.[21] Nishitani in effect argues that despite the influence of Eastern philosophy on Schopenhauer's thought, there is an extent to which he could not take the radical leap of letting go of Western philosophical attachment to beings, Being, and the self. For Nishitani, those attachments "cover over reality" through elision of a brutal fact. Reality is not only perfectly fine without us, but also perfectly fine without beings and Being.[22] Recall my earlier anecdote about my youngest child's existential realization of prior and eventual nonexistence. Nishitani argues that this underlying realization, often submerged in our subconscious and unconscious, is among the reasons why philosophy is insufficient for our search for meaning in life. Attached to beings, Being, and other forms of meditation, philosophy lacks commitment to the radicality of what we face. This is also why philosophy and theology are caught in some of the conundrums of theodicy we explored in previous chapters of this book. Investments in being, Beings, and personal deification all fail to address how they are sources of, in a word, evil. Schopenhauer was to some extent aware of this in his preference for compassion over moralistic models of ethical life. But the core problem, Nishitani argues, is in the ambiguity of life where birth is always simultaneously a form of death and the latter a form of birth.[23] The radical dimension of the child's consternation at the thought of nonexistence is, radicalized, the realization that nothing *had to come into being*. The radicality of reality beyond beings and Being Nishitani asks us to consider through the Sanskrit term *Śūnyatā* (emptiness so radical it transcends all). Nishitani argues that problems of history and time in Western philosophy are steeped in Being and personification, which is why they often collapse into theodicean rationalization or eschatology.[24] Freed from such attachments, human existence could move from *Saṃsāra* (wandering) to *nirvāṇa* ("quenching"). One could see the point of no-longer-wanting in the sense of no longer wandering since there is no longer need in *Śūnyatā*. *Nirvāṇa* does not appear or is achieved here through clinging to or pursuing it; it is instead dying of *Saṃsāric* life, the end of wandering.[25] In agreement with Weil, who argues that decreation releases us from our ego and opens us to others, Nishitani argues *nirvāṇa* exemplifies radical possibilities of freedom and equality through paradoxically not taking ourselves or everything else too seriously. Instead of the life to be judged at death, there is the radical contingency of life as well, which shifts from the drama of death. Life, in other words, is for living without fear of death.

In response to the question of a life worth living, Nishitani and Weil would remind us that those who have not measured up are no less deserving of life and, consequently, living.

Killing Humanity

Although we are all condemned to death, it makes all the difference to each of us whether that shared fate is something any of us, in our life story, deserves. Jaspers has written of this problem as *Die Schuldfrage* (the guilt/blame/responsibility question).[26] The term *Schuld* is related to the German word *Schule* (school), which reveals the pedagogical dimension of the concept. The notion of guilt without learning is pointless and, in many instances, pathological. Jaspers was thinking through the disaster wrought by the actions of the German government, many of the German people and their allies, and the general responsibility shared by German citizens leading up to, during, and after World War II. They left nations in ruins, and in some cases, given their genocidal intentions, suffering biocultural catastrophe, the result of which, although difficult to see today, was Germany seemingly left in ruins. Jaspers outlined four kinds of guilt with correlated responsibilities—metaphysical, ethical and moral, legal, and political. The first pertains to one's relationship with the Absolute or existence throughout the universe or pluriverse; the second is a relationship with the rules and mores of one's society and one's relationship with one's self; the third is a matter of positive law; and the last is the responsibility every member of a society has for the actions of its government. The last, as he addressed it to his fellow Germans at the end of World War II, raises the question of whether a people's government has acted in a manner that affords mercy in the instance of its defeat. Jaspers counsels every government to remember that it is the people, its citizens, who will suffer the debt, and in some instances the sentence of death, from such a trial. Returning to Schopenhauer and Ginsberg, if life is about preparing for not deserving to die, would it not be a catastrophe for a government or a society to have failed to offer the same for its people? Ginsberg admits:

> We are responsible for our extermination. Efforts exist to attribute the blame to the culprits among us: the rules, greedy, hostile, thoughtless, doctrinaire, military, otherworldly, Other. But they are our fellows. The blame is upon us for failing to control them or guide them to the light. Looking for a scapegoat, we also cast blame on the System, economic order, communication gap, uneven distribution of resources, violence of television, limitations of education, inhibitions of tradition, intolerance of religion. Yet, at heart, we know that human beings are victims of ourselves, not of circumstances. We allow circumstances and systems to get in our way.... The destruction of the world falls upon our head, if we fail to stop it.... You and I are obligated to save the world.... To be human requires action to save the world. Such action is without expectation of success. It need not be accompanied by hope.[27]

The concluding two sentences join us in the spirit of political commitment, the underlying theme of these reflections from the first onward. We come to the underlying theme, the one that stimulated the Freudian reflection and which is the animus for culture, the prosthetic god, which, as we know, needs to be fed and preserved because of the threat faced by all—namely, the ultimate catastrophe, not only the end of the world but also that of *all worlds.*

Empires, those mighty organizations that eroded national boundaries in their effort to achieve eternity through conquest, deceive their constituents with such a promise, which is achieved, no doubt, because many if not most people want to be deceived. Evidence, the remains of past empires, mock such fantasies, yet empires continue, and any society that achieves such continues to be beguiled by delusions of its own necessity. Take the United States from the 1950s up until 2016 as an example. Ask most—and, oddly enough, even many people from other countries up to that point—about what the demise of the United States would have meant, and they would have no doubt spoken honestly, though not truthfully: the end of the world. History has already revealed that, since the election of Donald Trump to the U.S. presidency, those from other countries have changed their position.

The world could, despite much ado, end not in a great cataclysm or hysterical action of an idiotic, mad, or group of mad Chief Executives but instead through a quiet and perhaps unnoticed whimper. The earlier meditations of culture pointed to a possibility suffered by many and forgotten by most. What can a society do when the sign continuum of the end of the world is the death of its form of culture?

The events since Christopher Columbus landed in the Bahamas in October 1492, inaugurating a period of expansion that transformed Christendom into

Europe and much of the rest of the world into colonies and most now former-colonies, include the rapid death of whole continents of peoples and their ways of life—the death, in other words, of worlds.[28] In many cases where the genetic material of the people survived, the symbolic life either disappeared or was mutated into a new kind of indigenous to the world constituted by new sets of relations. This struggle is not new, as similar questions marked struggles of similar kind in antiquity and even earlier, as a forgotten time of different *species* of hominins reveal. Neanderthals and Denisovans appear to us as fossilized zoological ruins, even though traces of them continue in the transformed populations we now know as Europeans, Asians, and descendants of sub-Saharan Africans who mixed with them. There are also cultural practices connected to whatever genetic adaptations they afforded with their descendants' environments. Although to some extent an "us" that is a new kind of "us," the basic conclusion remains that some genes remain where once robust cultural life of another kind existed. In relatively more recent times, Hellenic and then Roman civilizations offered for ancient Judeans the challenge of modernization, the result of which was the creation of Christianity and Rabbinic Judaism, the complex intellectual and spiritual struggle of reconciling the Hellenic, Roman, and Judean worlds, and a debate on the cultural location of Judaism to this day.[29] Similar concerns abound with regard to the place of the Arabic world in North Africa, the varieties of Mainland Northeast Asian civilizations on the Pacific islands, including the Indigenous peoples of what is today Japan. And in the project of the Americas imposed on Abya Yala, this problem of cultural disaster unfolded in the genocidal practices that reduced the numbers of Native populations through the cultural hegemony of Spain and Portugal in the South, and England and France in the north, with brief instances of Denmark and The Netherlands. There are still speakers of these colonized indigenous languages, but many fear, as speakers diminish even where the population (genetic material) continues, the looming cultural equivalence of the end of the world.

For some, cultural disaster takes the form of a ruined existence. There are, all over the world, people living through cultural ruin or culture on the verge of ruin. The struggle of continuation is Promethean. For some, the struggle for cultural continuity drags cultural practice out of the stream of mundane life to the level of sacrifice and fanatical devotion. Religious fundamentalisms are the perverse bedfellows of cultural preservation. How could certain cultural practices become relevant across all time without war in the future? If subsequent generations must be bound to past ones in an eternal circle of the same, would not the effect become one of never truly having been born? There are many myths about parents refusing the birth of the next generation. Among the Hellenic peoples, Ouranos (sky) refused to let his children emerge from the birth canal of their mother Gaia (earth). Kronos, one of the sons, took the option of castrating his father and throwing his genitals into the sea from which sprang Aphrodite. Among the Israelites, disobedience in the form of eating from the fruit of knowledge led to expulsion from paradise, and an endless chain of sacrifices of children to elders, which offers a narrative of election (to be chosen, *bakhir*) as the responsibility to preserve and protect the ethical expression of the *Imago Dei* on earth. There, prayers as sacrifice remind younger generations that theirs is to give, the giving, the commandments or *Mitzvot*. The holy source of giving also demands much. What happens to Judaism, many Jews worry in the wake of *Shoah* in World War II and the subsequent emergence of Israel, when generations emerge who wish no longer to give but to take?

Permanent Catastrophe in Human Terms

The youth are losing their youthfulness. For too many, the burden of living one's life is already unbearable. To add the weight of one's people and one's culture, as has been the lot of colonized peoples, beckons the dreaded tide of lost horizons. Exhaustion lurks.

Cultural disaster leads to a rallying of forces against the future. It demands sacrifice of the young. Some may point to the recent right-wing plea for the elderly to sacrifice themselves for the sake of protecting Capitalism during the COVID-19 pandemic as a counter argument. We should bear in mind that such claims were issued in bad faith, since it is primarily the younger generations, the poor, and the racially disadvantaged who would be forced to back into dangerous workplaces. The elderly—especially those affluent ones making such pleas—could just safely quarantine themselves away in retirement. Richard Fenn, in *The Secularization of Sin*, reads Euromodern burdens on the youth through ancient grammars of sacrifice devoid of their original telos or purpose.[30] Appealing to the Daedalus myth as inspiration, Fenn argues against institutions of authority that deploy mystifying practices to hold sway over the youth. This blocks possibilities, he contends, of growing into responsible adults. Daedalus was the gifted technician who built the labyrinth to hide away the Minotaur, the offspring of Pasiphaë's (King Minos's queen's) lusty union with the white bull given to Minos by Poseidon for sacrifice to the gods. Fenn reads the myth as a tale of insatiable greed with consequences so ugly that additional precautions of subterfuge were needed. Minos' greed led to his withholding the bull instead of returning it to the gods. To make matters worse, Pasiphaë's lust and greed were such that she masqueraded as a cow to satisfy her desire for union with the bull. The offspring, the Minotaur, born from greed, was cast into the labyrinth where he consumed those unfortunate enough to be lost there. These calamities did not abate Minos' deceitfulness and greed. Hoping for permanent access to Daedalus' technical genius, he imprisoned Daedalus and his son Icarus in a tower overlooking the sea. Daedalus then devised their escape by fashioning wings of feather and wax with which his son and he took flight over the open sea. Securing the wings with wax carried the danger of their melting when exposed to heat, so Daedalus warned Icarus not to fly toward the sun and not to fly close to the sea where he could be snatched by the violent waves. As we know with myth, Icarus stood no chance. He might as well have been Eve looking at the fruit of knowledge. Lost in the joys of flight, he flew too high, whereupon the sun's heat melted the wax and he plummeted down into the ravenous sea.

The myth of Daedalus, Fenn contends, offers a tale of sacrifice, purification, and pressures of older generations on the young. Icarus is warned by his father (no doubt appearing monstrous as an admonition) not to fly too high or too low but to follow him, as many exemplars of patriarchal authority, what Fenn calls the Daedalus Complex, do. Icarus' fall reveals two poles of "purification"—fire and water. Thus, there is the greed manifested in institutions of power, the king and the queen, which consumes the people, and then there is the sacrifice by which purification is sought for the debt of consumption.

One cannot help but think of the significance of soap and water after conducting errands, which mostly involved shopping, during the time of the COVID-19 pandemic. For every act of consumption, purification becomes a matter of life and death. In the Euromodern world, where the mythic foundations of rituals of purification have been lost to measures of accumulated monetary wealth, a legitimation crisis emerges for institutions that demand sacrifices of the people, especially across generations and across communities. The lives of many people were imperiled, after all, by national leaders who worried more about the economy than the health of their citizenry. They, thus, delayed making the necessary preparations for the pandemic.

Fenn reflects: "When the Minotaur is clearly the government or banking system, there is no abiding reason for either tribute or sacrifice. The Protestant miracle is that so many are still willing to make their sacrifices to the larger society."[31] Writing at the end of the Reagan era of unbridled greed, his ruminations portended the pyramid scheme behavior in the financial and real estate markets that led to the situation of world financial ruin by the end of the George W. Bush administration, which was rescued by the Obama administration, and then returning under the Trump administration. Trump's allies include authoritarian leaders of Brazil, India, Hungary, Russia, and many unsavory types more promising a return to a romanticized purity. The sacrifices to this delusion are many, and who else will inherit the trillions in debts, not only in the United States but also for others worldwide, but everyone else, especially subsequent generations? As greed spread to financial derivatives, where betting on the future led to debt beyond the imagination of the present, the possibility of human foreclosure is hardly a fantasy. For our purposes, the warning represented by economic monsters, which oddly enough in the age of neoliberalism is any form of socialism, democratic or limited, is the dimension of the self, of the avowed better system, pushed from sight into a maze of confusion similar to the financial instruments used to dupe much of the public worldwide. As things fall apart, further distance is placed from the self through claims of impurity; somehow, the system has been polluted and purification must be waged.

Overlooked in the inevitable search for culprits (it is always someone else's fault), Fenn observes, is the demise of the individual as person versus institutional actors—in other words, the human relation to human institutions. What many of those who selfishly took from the system and its various institutions knew was that the latter would sacrifice them at the slightest threat. They, as expendable, followed the paths against being swallowed up. "This leaves the individual as *person* a mere survivor of the labyrinth."[32] Purification demands rooting out purveyors of the pollution that has spread throughout the community, which in this case extends across the globe, and the expected rituals of cleansing, which in the past involved fire (burnings, electric chairs, dropping a few atomic and hydrogen bombs), water (drowning or rebirth through baptisms and conversions), or burial and resurrection (incarceration). The accused continue to be the usual suspects: immigrants (undocumented and otherwise), social pariah, and other members of the damned of the earth (Indigenous and racialized peoples). But those are ultimately not enough to erase the burden placed on those rendered distant in the obfuscation of global hysteria—namely, the young and subsequent descendants. "Any community that seeks to restore primordial unities, to pay the debt of the individual to those who have gone before and to the world itself," declares Fenn, "is inevitably going to stimulate demands for an unbroken harmony with both the natural and social orders. That harmony will always be threatened by the young and the old, by aliens and intruders, and by those who represent impurities in the ideological or social system."[33] What about those whose domain is the future? "Certainly the young, who like Icarus 'impede their fathers at their work' and seem to play when the serious rites of the community are at stake, can be scapegoated as a source not only of innovation but of threat to the community as a whole."[34]

There is something awry from the times of Fenn's reflections in the 1980s. There is, after all, a form of conservatism among a substantial number of the young. It takes the form of a desperate search for fathers, whether loving or abusive. It is not unnoticed that the turn to the right in the first quarter of the 21st century has taken the form, for the most part, of geriatric executive leadership making promises they could not possibly keep. Nowhere is this starker than in the United States, where Donald Trump and Bernie Sanders are iconic. There were voters in the 2016 election for whom psychological investment was for the left-wing Sanders and, failing that, the right-wing Trump. This absurdity becomes intelligible in psychoanalytical form. The mentality whose sense of security depends on having fathers instead of mothers—especially in a country obsessed with "Founding Fathers"—made the distinction between a loving father (Sanders) and an abusive, malignant narcissistic one (Trump) ultimately irrelevant. The situation in 2020 pretty much affirmed this point but with the addition of senility in a triumvirate of Biden, Sanders, and Trump. This is so despite a crucial point. The loving father, at least, thinks about the future. In psychoanalytical terms, he is willing to sacrifice himself for the children. It is significant that Daedalus did not fly down and attempt to rescue Icarus. In recent times, the tale is worse, where the leadership is more like Daedalus' kicking Icarus into the ocean so as to be relieved from the burden of looking out for him.

There is a yoking of the young brought to the understanding of debt and sacrifice. The next generation is, in effect, forced to be the parents of those from whom they have descended by virtue of the debts they bear. Beyond the constraints of economic ensnarement are the cultural presuppositions lived in each generation as though permanent. Implicit in such presumption is the same cultural fear pushed to subconscious levels of being indebted to the past but without a future. What else could the youth sense in such times, with fear and trembling, but the end of the world?

There is something to learn in this regard from dying cultures' struggles in relations of the old to the young. All cultures ultimately die, and their signals, as what Jane Anna Gordon and I call divine warnings, are for what all must learn. Despite avowed preservation for the sake of children and subsequent generations, the disaster of contemporary society, its sign continuum, is that by not facing our responsibilities we are ruining the future *as future* and are thereby making the case for what Jaspers lamented—namely, a deserved vanquishing of humankind.

It is stupid for humankind to expect to live forever. Schopenhauer, Ginsberg, and Fenn remind us that life as a preparation for death involves taking seriously what one must do for the sake of life. Yet the reader may already sense a tension in these reflections with the underlying theme of eliminating narcissistic self-investment. Writing on the great patriarch Abraham through the voice of Johannes Silentio, Kierkegaard offered this reflection: "… he who always hopes for the best becomes old, and he who is always prepared for the worst grows old early, but he who believes preserves an eternal youth."[35] Belief here also means faith. But it is not a naïve expectation. Although Kierkegaard was steeped in the concerns of the self, his insight, which guided many of my reflections on ethical and political commitment throughout these critical reflections, need not be placed in Christological and theistic form. Radicalized, it also points to Nishitani's understanding of *dharma* faith toward all life, which, as he characterized it, is an original vow marked by compassion.[36] The youthfulness of which Kierkegaard wrote is an understanding of what ultimately matters. On this, Nishitani and Weil would agree; life cannot be lived through fear of nor preparation for death. It is about not fearing death and in so doing being able to live life without our selves getting in the way. Taking life too seriously returns us to being gripped in the fear of death. A society that fails to understand such wastes what little time it has fortifying itself at the expense of others, including itself. Ignoring that is perilous. The testament to the unheeded warnings of our age may be an epitaph of admonition from desperate final efforts. The worst would be for the youth to suffer exhaustion from wasted energy, for they would no longer have anything to offer but the mark of the permanent catastrophe, through the absence of effort, of life unfortunately left foreclosed.

Notes

1. See G. Lemître, "The Beginning of the World from the Point of View of Quantum Theory," *Nature* 127 (9 May 1931): 706–706. http://www.nature.com/nature/journal/v127/n3210/abs/127706b0.html. For a detailed discussion of implications of quantum theory for social science, see Mohammad H. Tamdigidi, *From Newtonian Toward Quantum Imaginations: Volume 1, Undriddling the Quantum Enigma* (Belmont, MA: Okcir Press, 2020).

2. See his *Philosophy of Symbolic Forms, 3 vols.*, trans. Ralph Manheim (New Haven, CT: Yale University Press, 1953–1955), and for a contemporary discussion of the relevance of his approach, see Drucilla Cornell and Kenneth Panfilio, *Symbolic Forms for a New Humanity: Cultural and Racial Reconfigurations of Critical Theory* (New York, NY: Fordham University Press, 2010).

3. For a careful, methodic philosophical critique and discussion, see Kwasi Wiredu, *Cultural Universals and Particulars* (Bloomington, IN: Indiana University Press, 1996).

4. See Part I of Nietzsche's *Der Wille zur Macht. Versuch einer Umwerthung aller Werthe (Studien und Fragmente)*, Heinrich Köselitz and Elisabeth Förster-Nietzsche (Leipzig, Germany: C.G. Naumann, 1901), available in English as *The Will to Power*, trans. Walter Kaufmann and R. J. Hollingdale (New York, NY: Vintage, 1968).

5. See Nietzsche, *Zur Genealogie der Moral: Eine Streitschrift* (Leipzig, Germany: C.G. Naumann, 1887); availabe in English as *On the Genealogy of Morals* trans. Walter Kaufmann and R. J. Hollingdale (New York, NY: Vintage, 1989).

6. Jane Anna Gordon and Lewis R. Gordon, *Of Divine Warning: Reading Disaster in the Modern Age* (New York, NY: Routledge, 2009).

7. "Asteroid 2013TV135—A Reality Check," *NASA News* (17 October 2013): http://www.nasa.gov/mission_pages/asteroids/news/asteroid20131017.html#.U3rSiLyCpZk.

8. Robert Ginsberg, *The Aesthetics of Ruins* (Amsterdam, The Netherlands: Rodopi, 2004), 387.

9. See Freud, *Totem und Tabu: Einige Übereinstimmungen im Seelenleben der Wilden und der Neurotiker* (Leipzig, Germany: Hugo Heller, 1913; *Analysis of a Phobia on a Five-Year-Old Boy (Little Hans)* (London, UK: Hogarth Press, 1909); and *Moses and Monotheism*, trans. Katherine Jones (New York, NY: Vintage, 1954).

10. Nietzsche explores this in a variety of texts, but see his inaugural work, *Die Geburt der Tragödie aus dem Geiste der Musik* (Leipzig, Germany: E.W. Fritzsch, 1972).

11. Jean-Paul Sartre, *Being and Nothingness: A Phenomenological Essay on Ontology*, trans. with an intro. by Hazel Barnes (New York, NY: Washington Square Press, 1956), 584–585.

12. Originating in Buddhist thought (which encourages self-detachment in the form of not taking one's self too seriously), this concept followed a path through Arthur Schopenhauer and Nietzsche to its more systematical examination in Sartre's *Being and Nothingness* and Simone de Beauvoir's *The Ethics of Ambiguity*. I expanded this concept at the methodological level to problems of disciplinary formation, especially in the human sciences; see Lewis R. Gordon, *Disciplinary Decadence: Living Thought in Trying Times* (New York, NY: Routledge, 2006). Michel Foucault also explores this concept, although not explicitly so, in *Technologies of the Self: A Seminar with Michel Foucault*, Patrick H Hutton, Huck Gutman, Luther H. Martin (Amherst, MA: University of Massachusetts Press, 1988).

13. Ginsberg, *The Aesthetics of Ruins*, xvii.

14. *The Aesthetics of Ruins*, 7.

15. Arthur Schopenhauer, *The World as Will and Representation*, Vol. 2, trans. E.F.J. Payne (New York, NY: Dover Publications, 1958), 634–635.

16. *Ibid*, 637.

17. Ginsberg, *The Aesthetics of Ruins*, 419.
18. See Jacques Derrida, "La Pharmacie de Platon," in *La Disséminationtrans* (Paris, France: Éditions du Seuil, 1981).
19. Ginsberg, *The Aesthetics of Ruins*, p. 439.
20. *Ibid.*
21. Simone Weil, *Gravity and Grace*, trans. Emma Crawford and Mario von der Ruhr (New York: Routledge, 2002 [1947]), 78–80.
22. Keiji Nishitani, *Religion and Nothingness*, trans. Jan Van Bragt (Berkeley, CA: University of California Press, 1982), 16.
23. Ibid, 91.
24. Ibid, 209–215.
25. Ibid, 180.
26. See Karl Jaspers, *Die Schuldfrage. Von der politischen Haftung Deutschlands* (Munich, Germany: Piper, 1965), available in English as *The Question of German Guilt*, trans. E.B. Ashton (New York, NY: Fordham University Press, 2001).
27. Ginsberg, *The Aesthetics of Ruins*, 439.
28. Scholarship on the gravity of this catastrophe is copious. See, for example, Alvin M. Josephy, Jr., *America in 1492: The World of the Indian Peoples Before the Arrival of Columbus* (New York, NY: Vintage, 1993) and Russell Thornton, *American Indian Holocaust and Survival: A Population History since 1492* (Normal, OK: University of Oklahoma Press, 1990). And at the time of meeting, there are the words of the man himself: Christopher Columbus, *The Four Voyages of Christopher Columbus*, trans. J.M. Cohen. London, UK: Penguin Classics, 1992).
29. For a history of these dynamics from antiquity, see Shaye J.D. Cohen, *The Beginning of Jewishness: Boundaries, Varieties, Uncertainties* (Berkeley, CA: University of California Press, 1999).
30. Richard Fenn, *The Secularization of Sin: An Investigation of the Daedalus Complex* (Louisville, KY: Westminster John Knox, 1991).
31. Fenn, *The Secularization of Sin*, 163.
32. Fenn, *The Secularization of Sin*, 170.
33. Fenn, *The Secularization of Sin*, 178.
34. Fenn, *The Secularization of Sin*, 181.
35. Søren Kierkegaard, *Fear and Trembling*, Revised edition, trans. Walter Lowrie (Princeton, NJ: Princeton University Press, 2013), 50 (Danish Academy, iii, 71).
36. Nishitani, *Religion and Nothingness*, 26.

Epilogue

Conversation with Decolonial Philosopher Madina Tlotsanova on Shifting the Geography of Reason

MADINA TLOTSANOVA: Lewis, there are several concepts and ideas in your works that have had a great influence on me, changing my optics, methodological approaches, even the language of my own writing. Among them—disciplinary decadence, Existentia Africana, your take on "bad faith" departing from Sartre and through your dialogue with Fanon, your understanding of "problem people," etc. But perhaps the most important of your concepts is shifting the geography of reason. Undoubtedly, this is one of the key contemporary processes that is often blocked or opposed by those who do not want to allow such a shift. In Rolando Vazquez's terms, it would be a "humbling of modernity" with its specific narrow locality of knowledge production masked as universal yet excluding the majority of people as potential knowledge producers and as rational beings. Could you please unpack the concept of shifting the geography of reason a little bit more for the Russian audience?

LEWIS GORDON: To understand shifting the geography of reason, we must first consider what "geography of reason" is. Paths we take often take us to those we don't intend and could never initially imagine. When I had formulated this idea in the 1990s, I was building on Enrique Dussel's concept of "the underside of modernity." It struck me that there is a dialectical aspect of living or being located at the underside. If we look at history, those from the underside usually hold the key to the future. Those on the surface imagine themselves to be where humanity is going. When they fall, they often watch their world serving as the outline for another to come, and it is often one with which they do not identify. So, it struck me that each empire left its unique traces that were transformed. There were Roman roads and aqueducts. There were the Arab trade routes. Across Africa there were trade routes from Songhai and Mali. And more recently, there were the ocean routes of the Portuguese and Spaniards from which the Danes, Dutch, and British built their way. They built theirs on the outlines of those in Abya Yala (which they called the Americas), and the United States and former Soviet Union had emerged on the outlines of others. Why then, I asked, couldn't it be the case that shifts from sails, to steam engines, to oil and gasoline, to silicone and information technology not have their own outlines through which creative people from the South could articulate a different future? Part of the arrogance of all empires is that they imagine they could open doors that lead one-way. Doors and keys are more than we take them for, and they plus various pathways offer contexts through which imagination and deed could build a different and hopefully better kind of tomorrow—one premised, at least, on concrete manifestations of freedom.

The unexpected paths are the many discoveries along the way. Taking hold of building alternative futures requires a commitment to having a future at all. Where the geography of reason means that only certain groups of people, in a specific geopolitical location called the "North," have a future and reason, the structure of the relationship is reason supposedly coming "down" to the people of the "South." The implications are many. For example, the presumption is that people from the North offer through reason the ideas that make people of the South appear. Those from the South, thus, become passive recipients of such light. This, however, is a distortion of history and reality. It erases facts, and it cultivates dependency. It also leads, since the people of the North use reason to illuminate their experience, to the conclusion that Northern experience is more valuable than Southern ones. If the point is to bring reason to experience, then everyone must take responsibility for reason and the theory it creates. It is this *taking responsibility for reason* that leads to the shift. It is done *without permission* of those who attempt to horde reason. But here is the additional shift. The horded reason is a distorted reason. It is a form of unreasonable reason that imagines itself complete and standing on its own. Those who challenge it do so from an understanding of reason as an ongoing relationship and commitment to certain kinds of practices that are never "complete." Even the future is open. They, thus, in shifting the location/geography of reason, also shift reason itself from a closed to an open, relational commitment.

The implications of these shifts are many. They involve challenging even notions of "location." There are Southern elements in the geographical north—as we see in Eastern Europe and also the many migrant and refugee groups across the world—and there are Northern ones in the South, as we see with the disasters and coups and antidemocracy directions of privatization elites coopting countries such as Brazil and India. There is also the historical inheritance from colonialism, enslavement, and racism.

Another shift is the notion of "modern." The portrait I just gave reveals that to be modern—present—one must transform or shift one's understanding of belonging. One must belong to the future, which offers meaning to one's present and one's past. This means, then, if Europe is not *the future* but instead only a part of it, then the modern that has dominated the world for the past few hundred years is simply the "Euromodern." Understanding this is already a shift in the geography of reason. Indeed, it enables us to look at past moderns. If we were to use a time machine and go to the Mediterranean of antiquity and pick up some maps, we would have to turn some of them upside down to recognize the countries. Those maps reveal that people used to look "up" to the southern hemisphere. Africa was "above" what we now call Europe. Our world, then, is a transformation of one form of what was once modern for another, and we would be deluding ourselves if we were to think of the Euromodern as the last word on this process.

So, finally, if we think of my point about reason as an incomplete but ongoing commitment, we could see why I argued for *shifting*, instead of simply a shift, in the geography of reason. This shifting is a living, ongoing commitment to building livable worlds of living thought.

MADINA TLOTSANOVA: **What problems, issues, debates do you think are the most burning and crucial for contemporaneity? And generally, what is contemporaneity for you, how would you formulate its gist? Many of our European, American, and Russian colleagues of broadly leftist views are worried today about the rise of the ultra-right, conservative, and populist forces all over the world. But then is this really the gist of contemporaneity? How does the shift in the geography of reason correlate with this global rightist backlash?**

LEWIS GORDON: At the heart of contemporaneity is modern in the sense of a future worth fighting for. One of the signs of bankrupt positions is the need for them to hide under the guise of the new. In recent times, some intellectual movements promised emancipation, revolution, or at least a possibility of decency but were then revealed to be compatible with rendering their proponents defenseless under the growing onslaught of exploitation and disenfranchisement. Although having intellectual merit in its time, poststructuralism has now covered itself in the blanket of "critical theory" and there is oddly a version of it even in some forms of avowed "decolonial theory." This affected many kinds of left thought, where even the varieties of Marxism are full of reservations, and worse, as the growth of globalism premised on privatization wreaked havoc, many on the left abdicated the task of building globalism that places life and people first. Romanticized localisms were coughed up as though human beings could return to a time in which we were unaware of or without contact with each other. The right was aware of this, and they knew that their nakedness offered a world that was, as the English philosopher Thomas Hobbes put it, "nasty, brutish, and short." So, they, too, covered themselves, although instead of a blanket, they used a white sheet. So, fascism, with all its racist, xenophobic, and reductive class elements—we should remember that the 21st-century fascists claimed they were fighting for the common (white) man—became "alt-right" and now even "ultra-right." Yet they are different. After all, the old fascists and right claimed to be offering imperial glory to last a thousand years. Today's fascists assert themselves in a world of political nihilism. That's what actually makes them scarier. Despite their bombasity, they don't actually believe in a future in the long-term sense. Theirs is an immediate future, which collapses into expecting everything for themselves in their lifetime. With that mentality, there is no room for the genuinely political. In fact, political life, with its demands of long-term commitment, becomes the enemy, which is why democracy is imperiled. To work with people reaches beyond the self to those who are ultimately anonymous.

A shift in the geography of reason requires thinking anew and creatively how we understand concepts such as "right" and "left." There are left-wing positions that can slide into the right when we understand their goals. After all, conservatism is a turn toward a past, a cherry-picked past, of supposed security, law and order, perfection. This often requires eliminating sources of dissent such as difference, creativity, and freedom—of which Hobbes was aware—and if pushed to its extreme offer fascism. We should understand that our world is not like those of the past. Too many people respond to these crises through trying to figure out which past century to which they belong—the 20th, 19th, or 18th. Our world is undergoing its own seismic shifts; with several billion people and technologies that traverse distances in a Nanosecond, we live in a smaller world and, thus, a smaller planet. We are compressing reality and, thus, imploding life. Thus, instead of one, burning question, there are many ranging from how to address a planet incapable of sustaining the kind of life to which past ages have committed us—and those who wish to return are condemning us—to, as the East Indian philosopher Sri Aurobindo put it, opening up our minds to our potential to address our challenges. The late political theorist Benjamin Barber put it this way: "Nature doesn't negotiate." We must understand that the challenges we face today are human produced; they are manifestations of power by which human beings could affect life beyond ourselves. That means they require human action for their transformation, and the human world of produced power is called politics. The right's effort to eliminate political life imperils us all, but we cannot address such a challenge through leaving the understanding of power, as has occurred with "global," in their hands. They assert power as exclusively coercive. It would be a mistake for the rest of us to adopt such a view. Coercive power disempowers. To fight against disempowerment requires empowerment. Shifting the geography of reason requires understanding power should not be reduced to a single element but instead should be explored in its creative potential. If we think of power as the ability to make things happen and securing access to the conditions of doing so, there is much proverbially to be done. If we think of the work to be done simply as that of elimination, of reaction, to the right, however, our course could lead to a form of anarchy in which we become small, privatized sites of protection: in short, a left that becomes the right. We need a responsible form of practice attuned to the many dimensions of what we are and our relationship to other forms of life. We need to unleash our capacity to create, to build meaning while being sober to the realities of the terrestrial creatures we are. This requires not only a shift in the geography of reason but also an understanding of what it means to be specks of dust on a speck of dust in a cloud of dust in a larger constellation of dust in a vast universe through which our future depends on our understanding that our little speck of dust is our world reaching out for others and also dependent, in the end, on each other.

In my writings, I argue this requires also a shift in our understanding of responsibility. Much of our planet is locked in the language of legal and moral responsibility and then metaphysical ones appealing to deities. We need to understand the uniqueness of political responsibility, which, as my good friend, the late Iris Marion Young, always stressed is about the future. And since I have argued that political life always addresses those who are anonymous—the not yet born and many among those who have become ancestors—we should understand what it means to fight for what is not about us individually but instead about what depends on us while transcending us. We often forget: each of us is a descendant of those who not only stood upright and developed tools and language but also realized the importance of non-narcissistic love.

MADINA TLOTSANOVA: **Many of us have given up on the university as a failed modern institute of knowledge production and distribution. It seems that the shift in the geography of reasoning would come not from academics, philosophers, or any institutionalized intellectuals who have long lost our impact on the society. Rather this shift would come from the fissures, interstices, and border spaces of negotiation which have never been seen before as sites of knowledge production—from bottom-up social movements, from art, music, literature, etc. In your view, what are the ways, tools, and spaces for shifting the geography of reason and who are its agents?**

LEWIS GORDON: I reject zero-sum arguments. The truth is we don't have advanced knowledge. We must strive to shift the geography of reason at every front. Intelligence and creativity are our greatest assets and we should use them. There is no greater enemy than the mixture of stupidity and pride. I, as you know, am not a disciplinary nationalist. I also reject the idea of the university as the sole province of the production of knowledge. In fact, it is part of the market colonization of politics to corner knowledge producers through making the university their only site of production. It transforms producing knowledge from a calling and makes it exclusively into a job. At this point, the threat of unemployment becomes the surest way of closing off revolutionary thought.

So, yes, you are right; shifting the geography of reason also requires shifting the geography of knowledge production. A shift, we should also bear in mind, does not mean abandonment. Academic knowledge has offered many gifts to our species, and at times it has even saved other forms of life. Our mistake is to leave such a grand and perhaps sacred task only in the hands of the academy. Academics who truly wish to learn should continue to be students, which means they should seek learning wherever they could find it. This counsel applies to everyone in pursuit of knowledge, wisdom, and other forms of learning, which means they should transcend themselves. They should continue to grow. In my book *Disciplinary Decadence*, that was the argument I advanced. We should not fetishize ourselves, disciplines, and methods of learning. We should be willing to go beyond them for the sake of things that matter, things greater than ourselves, such as reality, and even, paradoxically, our love for each other, since love is not only an embrace but also a letting go through a profound respect and empathy for freedom.

MADINA TLOTSANOVA: **To me, one of the main sensibilities of contemporaneity is the loss of the future dimension on a global scale. This "defuturing," to quote Tony Fry, is what we all share, and none of the contemporary political projects, ideologies, or philosophies seems to be able to offer an antidote for this futureless ontology. The sense of the lost future dimension is particularly acute in the post-Soviet countries that lost their radical utopian and forced progressivist vector overnight and were not offered any alternatives except going back to the end of the line and starting from scratch. Three decades later this peculiar sensibility of the post-Soviet "problem people," who were bypassed by history, is easily manipulated through various revanchist pseudo-Soviet or pseudo-national projects which once again look to the past and not to the future. What is your take on this issue? Do you think there is a future for this world? And what should be done to give the world back its future dimension or perhaps many intersecting future dimensions?**

LEWIS GORDON: This wonderful question pretty much summarizes my responses to the previous three questions. To it, I would add that you have identified a bad faith form of contemporaneity. It is the immediacy that collapses into the *"me"* as I identified as part of the mentality of the right and against which I voiced concern as it is being adopted by elements of the left. It is bad faith because it requires lying to the self about return and immediacy and about what the issues are. "Me" at the expense of all others leads, ultimately, to failures of the self. We already know this script, since there is no instance of any right-wing regime being able to sustain itself beyond a few generations. This is because too many resources are required to block the aspirations of a meaningful life. Given today the amount of energy consumed by human beings closest to the centers of consumption, the proverbial writing is already on the wall.

A critique of past futurism is the false dilemma of utopia versus dystopia. It is the mantra of the character Killmonger in the movie *The Black Panther*: conquer or be conquered. That movie is also an allegory with this response: why not find a way beyond conquest? A world without conquerors and conquered, without conquering, would not be a utopia. It would just be a better world. Here we come to another realization of shifting the geography of reason. Since it is in the present participle—about *doing, changing, building, etc.*—it makes reason also about reasoning, which means it is never ideal but instead about reasonability.

With regard to "problem people," I see that as connected to the ongoing logic of theodicy, where a god is rationalized as all good through making evil and injustice external to it. When it is secularized, it makes a society so, which means it blames its contradictions on those who suffer from it. And where the self becomes a god, the same logic follows.

An additional thing to consider is that much of this also emerges from two striking fallacies masqueraded as political life. The first is the notion of perfect people. Its logic is that somewhere out there is a set of people who got "it"—whatever the "it" is that we seek—*right*. Find them, imitate them, and we are good to go. It's even better when we supposedly are them. The second is that we can achieve anything if we have a big enough crowd. In our world of optics and showmanship, the right achieves this audibly through making the loudest noise. The cacophony offers the illusion of size, and those who find size attractive will join them. The clearly scary thing about these two fallacies is that they are attractive to the full range of the political spectrum.

MADINA TLOTSANOVA: **Although I am entirely for shifting the geography of reasoning, I am also aware of the fact that in some places and contexts it is too easy to misinterpret this decolonial gesture and let it be appropriated by reactionary forces. For example, in Russia, the appropriation of such rhetoric often takes place through neo-imperial channels and utilizes the imperial difference or, in other words, the continuing imperial rivalry. For the last several centuries, Russia has been marked by this peculiar inferiority complex vis-à-vis the West, which has often resulted in a too zealous copying and reinstatement of the dominant geography of reasoning (with a secret and futile hope of being eventually offered a place there, too). The anti-Western imperial discourses were by default formulated as either carving a better space in the global hierarchy or, in more radical cases, as** dismantling the existing hierarchy and building a new one with Russia in its center. The contemporary official anti-Western sentiment in Russia and a number of other post-Soviet and post-Socialist countries often appropriates elements of decolonial and postcolonial discourses. It is possible that the shift in the geography of reasoning can be also appropriated by these populist, nationalist, and imperial revivalist forces. In this situation, many critical minds opt for a liberal and hence, to some extent, pro-Western position and automatically reproduce the same modern/colonial geography of knowledge. In the present situation, this often looks like the only accessible protesting position. I am not happy with either of these stances (as they say in Odessa, "both are worse"), but then the question is: is there a way out of this binarism—either neo-imperial anti-Western nationalism or derivative liberal thought? And if and how can we defend our ideas and values from such an appropriation?

LEWIS GORDON: I am a critic of the term "appropriation." The human world of meaning is communicable, which means people could participate in many elements and also distort them. I take your use of the verb "to appropriate" to mean something like hijacking a term for misguided purposes, which also include erasing its history—as is what actually happens in processes of whitewashing history, for example. One of the things the right has always known is that ideas for a humane future often lack material capital with which to present their position as normative. Investment in alternative sites and rebranding them could be quite effective. Thus, there are those among the right-wing in the USA who call themselves "revolutionaries." This also happens all over Europe, and it is so in parts of Africa and Asia. What's more, the imperial reach of capitalism is such that even revolution, decoloniality, and shifting the geography of reason could be commodified in the way icons of the past ranging from Marx to Lumumba to Fanon to Guevara could be placed on T-shirts and worn by the very kind of people who would have ordered their assassination. There is no guarantee for what our ideas will unleash. We must have the integrity, if that were to come, to fight that as well. This was Fanon's point about decolonization. The skill-set of those who decolonize a society may not be the best ones for building its future. To maintain their legitimacy, those decolonizers could end up yoking their society to the always-presence of colonization. They then become those who must be overcome. I regard shifting the geography of reason as a task that, where healthy, creates possibilities. It is, however, a possibility of human reality. It becomes a mission, then, to be proverbially realized or betrayed. The political issue, as I have been arguing, is about the commitments of those who understand its importance without guarantees. As shifting the geography of reason is part of this ongoing struggle, it could also open the door for different kinds of struggles to come, including nefarious forces of misrepresenting it. We should remember, for instance, that "freedom" is a word that suffers from similar challenges. There are those who use the term to block it. It is important, for those of us committed to doing otherwise, to use it, or at least through engaging in necessary practices, to liberate it.

It is odd that the Euromodern advancement of liberal theory, which I regard as ultimately subordinating politics to morality and individualism as part of the philosophical anthropology of capitalism, has so many of us stuck in a binary emerging from the seating of the Monarchists and the republicans in the French parliament. Some of the ways I have been talking about the right and the left is to make more fluid our understanding of these concepts and for us to consider ways of thinking about the future beyond right-wing immediacy or rejection, liberal centrism, libertarian left anarchism, and end of history utopianism. It occurs to me that we need also to move beyond such decadence and begin the work of producing kinds of actions premised on our being the conditions of different kinds of "we" who may, should they look back at us, consider themselves fortunate, though their lives may be beyond our understanding. On this matter, I share Frederick Douglass's, Simone Weil's, and the Pakistani political theorist Asma Abbas's understanding of such work as not only political responsibility but also a peculiarly political form of love.

Index

CPSIA information can be obtained
at www.ICGtesting.com
Printed in the USA
LVHW081030120123
737030LV00021B/291